I0491518

BUSINESS START-UP MANUAL

A Practical Guide for Entrepreneurs

Omar Javaid

KDP Direct Publishing

Business Startup Manual: A Practical Guide for Entrepreneurs

Copyright © Omar Javaid, 2020

First published 2020 by KDP Direct Publishing

ISBN 9798671047998

Edited and typeset by the Author

The right of Omar Javaid to be identified as the author of this work has been asserted in accordance with the Copyright, Designs and Patents Act, 1988. All rights reserved.

No part of this publication may be reproduced, stored in a retrieval system, or transmitted, in any form or by any means (electronic, mechanical, photocopying, recording or otherwise), without the prior written permission of the publisher.

This publication is designed to provide accurate and authoritative information. It is sold under the express understanding that any decisions or actions you take as a result of reading this book must be based on your judgement and will be at your sole risk. The author will not be held responsible for the consequences of any actions and/or decisions taken as a result of any information given or recommendations made.

Cover designed, printed and bound by KDP Direct Publishing

About the Author

Dr. Omar Javaid has a Phd in Entrepreneurship from Institute of Business Management, MS in Management Sciences from KIET, MBA (executive) from IoBM with majors in Marketing, and BE in Industrial & Manufacturing Engineering from NED University. Mr. Javaid's core competence is mentoring new startups, and ventures; since 2010 he has helped hundreds of students in their entrepreneurial ambitions. He has also been empowering students to set up micro businesses for poor unemployed folks, and have successfully initiated around 500 such projects during the last 10 years. Mr. Javaid has been invited to speak multiple times at IBA, NED University, UIT, NEST I/O, and SoL on topics related to entrepreneurship. He has also published various research articles, and editorials in various journals, magazines, and newspapers;, and is a reader of Entrepreneurship, Social Entrepreneurship, Islamic Economics, and Finance, and Philosophy of Economics, and Business Management. Apart from teaching at IoBM he is also responsible to mentor IoBM students to set up entrepreneurial ventures, and facilitate in the process of developing an entrepreneurial ecosystem within the Institute.

Twitter: @javaidomar
FB: drjavaidomar

The following students of MBA executive at IoBM has contributed in producing some chapters in part 3 of this document, their names are also mentioned in footnotes of their respective chapters in part 3 of the document:

- Muhammad Salman Farooq
- Shamsher Ali
- Nabeel Azeem
- Razi Uddin
- Faizan Abdul Khaliq
- Zaid Hanif

Please share any suggestions to fix, improve, amend, simplify, elaborate, enhance, and enrich the content in this manual on omarjavaid@outlook.com

Table of Content

Part – 1

What & Why of Entrepreneurship

Chapter 1...

Why Entrepreneurship should be a Preferred Career Choice?

I have been asked often why I promote entrepreneurship to an extent that I don't even give career guidance to employment seekers ... Answer: Entrepreneurship creates employment, and to know the importance of entrepreneurship you need to imagine the pain, humiliation, and misery experienced during unemployment ... being unemployed is a horrifying experience, to know it, you have to experience it God forbid ..., and it gets even frightening when you have a family dependent on you ... often we hear about individuals committing suicides, killing their children, or giving them to orphanage houses, let alone selling them in the market, etc. as it is too difficult to bear the pain and anxiety of seeing your loved ones going hungry because you are out of work ... It is a little surprising why employment is one of the topmost crucial problems of modern macroeconomics theory, the other one being inflation.

Promotion of Entrepreneurship has a way out from this crisis ... entrepreneurship is about creating new businesses, and the success of a new business typically creates (self-)employment at least for the entrepreneur. It is quite likely that they create employment for others as well in this process ... consider an example of a vegetable cart, which can generate employment for at least three to four individuals (check this when you buy vegetables next time from a proper roadside vendor) ...

The educated, able, skilled lot of this country if encouraged to start small, and medium-sized businesses, will not just be beneficial for them but also for a lot more people.

My confidence in this solution to a painful economic problem of unemployment is reinforced with a saying of Prophet Muhammad (P.B.U.H) that the *Rizq* provided by Allah s.w.t is distributed among people such that its 9/10 parts go to businessmen or traders, and 1/10 parts go to the employed ... It is like saying that a building has 10 rooms, each having the same opportunities, but if 100 people want to get in any particular room then obviously space is not enough for everyone to fit in, on the contrary, if they decide to explore other rooms as well, then everyone will find enough space ...

There is another reason to talk about entrepreneurship. Local business development reduces the reliance of the economy from foreign MNCs. It is a myth that MNCs help local economies grow ... unfortunately, this false notion is believed by our educated class; many business students raise this question 'what about the employment generated by these MNCs'? That's a question asked in isolation, MNCs do not just create employment for a few, but along the way, they also put lots of other local firms out of business (though this might not always happen) henceforth as result the employment in an economy may not increase. The sole motive of an MNC is to generate ROI; if it invests say $1 million, it will take away for example $1.1 million or more from a particular economy leaving it worse off in the end. MNCs also attempt to manipulate the entire socioeconomic, and political structure of a country as a whole depending upon the extent of its operations. Social disintegration (which may also lead to mental health issues, and suicide), rise in inequality, unemployment, environmental degradation, contamination of land, and water with hazardous chemicals, human rights violations, the financial backing of corrupt regimes, etc. have been reported in many third world countries around the globe due to the direct or indirect influence of MNCs.[1] A total of $1.7 trillion worth of value is taken away annually by MNCs from the third world countries as per some estimates via stealing raw material, and tax evasions as per Laurence Cockcroft (as explained in his book 'Global Corruption).

Having said that local entrepreneurial development can reduce the reliance of an economy from MNCs, but that's possible only if entrepreneurial ventures are encouraged, and those who have the potential may realize their responsibility to go for it[2]... Our education system from the very start keeps conditioning the students to become an employee. Many who can become entrepreneurs are forced by the conditioning at school, and even family to become employees rather. However in South Asia for example members of various communities like Pathan, Memon, Chinioti, Dawooodi Bohra, Delhiwala, Gujrati, Ismaili, etc. communities are still saved from such a trend (this may not be true for their upcoming generations); as most of them raise their kids to be business-minded, and formally educate them to the extent necessary to manage their family businesses (see Appendix 1, and 2 for more details). The businesses in Pakistan (for example) are perhaps growing to the extent to which these communities are growing. The rest of the population may also need to take charge before it's too late.

---

[1] Anyone looking for details shall go through Naomi Klein's book, and documentary 'The Shock Doctrine', Noam Chomsky's articles, and books on globalization (Google them), John Grey's book 'The False Dawn', Mark Achbar's documentary 'The Corporations', various documentaries by Michael Moore etc etc … (Disclaimer: this is my personal analysis, not the official position of the intuition I work for, and I intend not to generalize all MNCs as bad, there may be exceptions as well)

[2] Local law, and order conditions, and a sense of security in the market are however a prerequisite, ensuring of which in fact is a job of the state

The business schools can help here, instead of creating employees for MNCs, and Banks, they need to realize their social responsibility as well, and begin to inspire, and train their graduates to become entrepreneurs instead. Various universities are now thinking on these lines. Some of them are not just teaching entrepreneurship in theory, but also helping students to experiment in real-time. Holistically speaking the idea is to create an ecosystem, an environment conducive for students who aspire to be entrepreneurs or start their own little business in real life. Once a critical mass of students is on it the idea would become contagious.

What's the best time to start a Business

You might have to ask this question if you do not belong to a business-oriented family ... The answer is simple: the best time to start a business is when you are studying!!! Why? because this is the time you have the luxury to experiment a lot, take a few risks, without much pressure; and with a little common sense, and smart thinking, you can avert yourself from making a loss, let alone making enough for your pocket money ... On the other hand, when you graduate, the pressure from your family or in-laws to get a good job will hardly let you experiment, let alone becoming an entrepreneur. From there onwards it will only become more difficult with the perpetual addition of family responsibilities, and liabilities as you become a spouse, then a parent, so on, and so forth.

There is another reason for it. Your education would mold you into a conformist employee depending upon how seriously you take your grades ... It is not impossible to think about entrepreneurship, or self-employment after completing your education, however, the chances will gradually decrease with the time you spend studying, unless you are exceptional, and have not allowed the conditioning at your school to transform you into a tool of the corporate machinery!!!...

So buckle your seat belt, and give it a try, as no wonder, with little perseverance, common sense, interpersonal skills you might end up establishing your own business, and become financially independent... on the other hand becoming an employee will only limit you to the boundaries provided by your working environment, for entrepreneurs, there are no such boundaries...

If you initiate a start-up while you are studying business for e.g, you will not be only studying theory but also will be practically applying it in your venture ... My personal experience shows that such students perform just as good as others, perhaps sometimes even better, thanks to the practical application of the theory they are studying (this has been also observed by Kiran Sethi's experiment at RiverSide School in India). It is needless to mention that such an experience nevertheless gets students ahead from the rest in terms of maturity, practical knowledge, and self-confidence.

There is a catch however, the curriculum, and pedagogy in business schools are not designed to bring up entrepreneurs, rather good employees, managers for large corporations[3]. Therefore students at present have to recontextualize the conventional theory to make it useful for the application.

In short, starting your own business, irrespective of how much profit it generates while you are a student, will not enrich your learning experience but also will introduce a much more lucrative, and enriching career option

---

[3] See Steve Blank's lecture: Democratization of Entrepreneurship on https://youtu.be/n-H7TAcqGko

in your life, i.e. of becoming an Entrepreneur. See Appendix 1 for more insights.

It may be argued that at the age of 18 or 20 one may not be mature enough to start a business or lack experience, and many reports about the age of successful entrepreneurs in the so-called developed part of the world suggest that one must be at least in his or her 40s to be able to successfully start a venture. This may not be true for new entrepreneurs belonging to entrepreneurial communities like Memon, Delhiwala, Chinioti, Gujrati, Ismaili, etc. perhaps because of the kind of upbringing they have received. Jared Diamond has also argued that the kind of upbringing strategies common in the western world delays the sense of internal security, and maturity among people, while in traditional tribes in places like Papua New Guinea, such a delay is not observed.

Nevertheless, even if you at the age of 25 do not feel mature enough or confident enough, or have not received the necessary upbringing which could enable you to start a business, which essentially is an act of managing the relationship with all stakeholders, then you may start small as take baby steps, do small experiments, just start by selling some basic stuff among your friends, and family, and gradually try to experiment your way up into complexity, and scale. Remember, persistence is the key, and persistence would come from 'why' you want to start your own business in the first place, and if you aren't sure, then you may start your journey through introspection, and self-exploration, by asking yourself 'why' you want to do anything. Also remember, honesty with yourself, self-respect, and self-awareness are among your greatest assets.

Chapter 2...

Financial Capital vs. Entrepreneurs

More than often, when I try to motivate undergraduate, and executive students toward entrepreneurship, they complain about the lack of capital, which they argue is necessary to start a business. Asking for capital without experience, without necessary execution skills, without a workable idea, etc., is like asking for a sports car, without knowing how to drive (in traffic in particular), and without knowing where to go. Even a layman can anticipate what would happen eventually. My doctoral research, my experience of working with entrepreneurs, and previous literature suggest that access to capital from an institutional investor, in particular, can do more harm than good for inexperienced entrepreneurs (angle investment is a better option, but please wait for a moment). This may sound counterintuitive, particularly when traditional textbooks on entrepreneurship tell you to make a business plan to convince a bank or a VC when the government. initiatives exclusively talk about the investment to promote entrepreneurship, and when every incubation center incubates its start-ups to make them look attractive to potential investors. Money is generally believed to be the most important ingredient of an entrepreneurial process.

Experience and recent research on real entrepreneurs suggest otherwise. The availability of cash coupled with inexperience or immaturity often leads to unproductive expenditure. Wasting money on lavish office space and unnecessary staff are common examples. It typically requires sufficient experience, emotional maturity, and wisdom to see which of the running or fixed expenses can lead to positive cash flow. Even if the expenses are meticulously managed, customer behavior is often unpredictable, so major changes in the imagined-value-proposition are often required to find the correct sweet spot. So the cash flow may not emerge as mentioned in the business plan, this may increase the chance of failure if a chunk of investment money is already spent on unnecessary ego-boosting stuff. Every act which may end up inflating the ego, like impressing investors or setting up a nice office space, can reduce the possibility of success.

Contrary to inflating their ego, entrepreneurs need the humility of a Level Five Leader (see Jim Collins), and agility to quickly adapt to changing market scenarios or new market insight. Traits like Humility, and agility unfortunately do not emerge when you take a route toward institutional investment with a business plan in your hand. Humility can be misinterpreted as a sign of weakness by the investors. Further, an investor's overarching influence may even cripple the ability to rapidly adapt to developing scenarios. Agility is dependent on strong intuition (see Ricardo Semler, and Nick Hauner), as there is often not enough time to scientifically gather data, and perform complex data analysis before making a decision (let alone the accuracy of the scientific process). However, using intuition is also counterintuitive for institutional investors who only understand the language of scientific analysis. Therefore, there is a heavy unquantifiable price to pay to attract investment, which often cripples an entrepreneur's ability (humility to accept mistakes, agility, and intuition to quickly adapt) to walk on an unpredictable-nonlinear spiral-like path of establishing a venture.

What to do?

Sara Sarasvathy, Carl Schramm, Ricardo Semler, Jim Collins, Alexander Osterwalder, Steve Blank, David Gerber (just to name a few), my doctoral research, and experience with entrepreneurs in Pakistan suggests an alternative route. To begin with, it is fundamentally necessary to gain industry experience, execution skills, emotional maturity, and wisdom. Or start something which one can manage with an available set of skills. The best way to gain the necessary experience according to Jack Ma (Founder Alibaba) is to work for a few years for a small or medium-sized business under a good boss. Carl Schramm, entrepreneur, and former chairman of Kauffman Foundation, also shares his similar observation in his book 'Burn the Business Plan'. This is a standard practice among Ethnic Entrepreneurial Communities (EEC) like Memon, Delhiwala, Chinioti, Bohri, or Ismaili. So before worrying about finding investment at first, potential entrepreneurs need to worry about how much experience they have. If more than one partner intends to start a business, some of them need to have the necessary market experience and execution skills.

It is interesting to note that the age of successful entrepreneurs in the USA is between 42 to 46 years (Ref. World Economic Forum). By this time they have already worked for someone, developed their network (another fundamentally important resource), gained necessary skills, and experience, gained market knowledge, industry insight, and realized a potential market gap that needs to be filled. Carl Schramm even argues that big firms are the best incubators for new start-ups, while actual incubators in Schramm's view have done more harm than good to the growth of entrepreneurship. Real growth requires real stressors according to Nassim Nicholas Taleb, which an entrepreneur experiences in real market conditions, while a cozy, and protective atmosphere inside typical business incubation centers may do otherwise.

So it is best to grow organically (slow, and steady) while getting exposed to the heat in a real market environment, while bootstrapping, reinvesting your profits, or at the least involving an angel investor only after you have stabilized the new venture. For example, if you want to locally manufacture UPS, and have the necessary technical skills at hand, but no market experience or capital, it is better to start with offering a repair service in a freelancing capacity. Establish a customer base gradually, and add the option of retailing an already available product to your clientele, if you don't have space to open a shop, selling online would do. The goal is to expand your customer base and establish trustable relationships with them. Once there are enough customers, you may think of backward integration by assembling the UPS, and then proceed toward manufacturing components one by one. This entire process may take 5 to 10 years. So the idea is to start simple, move slowly, while gaining experience, just like a plant grows naturally, spreading its roots deep in the ground, and gradually increasing in the complexity of operations as your experience, skills, maturity, market knowledge grows. Community networks with high social capital (typically found in EEC) are perhaps the best natural, and conducive environments to grow a venture through bootstrapping.

It is good to have a mentor to seek advice to avoid major pitfalls during a bootstrapping process; however, mentors have their limitations. Can an experienced driver give you instructions on the phone every second about how to drive a sports car in traffic, when you don't have much experience yourself? Would you be successful in reaching your destination? It is not very difficult to answer this question. If you are lucky enough to find an honest-concerned-mentor, he or she may give you some broad guidelines, help you set your direction, and align your steps. But you will have to figure out the micro details in your daily routine yourself, and it is in these details where you see the dance of the devil (referring to the idiom: 'the devil is in the detail').   Mentors advise, or advice from books on entrepreneurship, etc. can help to an extent. How many books will be required to learn the skill to survive in the wild like Bear Grylls (host of the Discovery TV show: Man vs. Wild)? According to Richard Branson, it is better to work for an expert as a helper to learn the desired skills. Once the skills are acquired, books my help.

Mentors are often busy people, you will be lucky to catch an hour every week with them. However working for a boss who is interested in developing your skills is a better alternative, as mentioned above. There is a saying in Urdu that 'kharbooza kharboze ko dekh ke rung pakarta hai', so if you have five friends for example, who are entrepreneurs, then your chances of ending up as an entrepreneur are high. I believe that members of EEC are not born entrepreneurs, it's just they see so many entrepreneurs around them while they grow up, and when they see a few failures in their circle, their orientation often shifts towards building a career as a professional, working for someone else.

Your immediate, and extended circle is perhaps a greater resource than capital. As from this network, if you have the right kind of connections, you do not just take aspirations, and advice, but also find your first customers, suppliers, employees, even angel investors. Such utilization of resources in one's network is common in EEC. If your network does not give you access to such stakeholders it is better to work hard in upgrading your network, even if you have sufficient capital in your pocket. Your network in actual is your net worth (see Porter Gale). Building it however takes years, as people who would like to become your first customers, suppliers, or even angel investors must already consider you a credible person having sufficient potential. That's where spending time in the market becomes fundamental, which should start at the age of 14, and above so that when you complete your education you already have sufficient experience, and connections with the right people to start something on your own. This practice is already common among members of EEC, where children spend their free time in their father's or relative's business particularly during their summer vacations. Contrarily job oriented families see it as a hindrance in receiving a proper education to secure a job that may not exist. (Space constraints limit me to share more, please see my articles on LinkedIn for further discussion)

Financial Capital vs. Innovative Ideas

To experiment with any new kind of innovation, one must already have a running business. Contrarily, what Mark Zuckerberg did is not normal. One has to be extremely lucky to hit a jackpot as 99.9999% entrepreneurs who start their business, do not follow the route which the likes of Zuckerberg have been able to take. Unfortunately most people in the modern start-up culture attempt to follow the line. The trend is even endorsed by financial markets resulting in start-ups that are only created to be sold to an investor or attract multiple series of investments. The value proposition is created less for the end-user, and more for the investors. It is typically the IT-based ventures which focus on gathering as many users as possible by providing something of entertainment value (FaceApp is a recent example). The number of users on their app or website thus determines the worth of their venture. Often the service is provided free of cost or at subsidized rates to get as many customers as possible. The money is not made through selling a product or a service, but by finding the next series of investments. Every new investor bails out the previous one. Uber and Twitter for example are still not in profit as of now, while their shareholders earn through capital gains only. Such unicorns blur the difference between a stock market, and a casino. The trend, unfortunately, has corrupted new venture creation according to Tim O' Reilly (the man behind the terms 'Open Source', and 'Web 2.0') as many start-ups now focus on creating a huge user base without providing meaningful value. As a result, impending societal problems that prevail in our food chain, health care industry, or global problems like climate change, etc. remain ignored by typically by new entrepreneurs or investors. Chamath Palihapitiya, CEO of Venture Firm 'Social Capital' is another concerned voice, who now only invests in ventures which create genuine value for the public by addressing the impending societal issues.

Pakistan's emerging entrepreneurial ecosystem is also not free from the potentially-corrupting influence of venture funds. Almost every incubation center in the country expects its start-ups to exit after being acquired by an investor. Acquisitions are often celebrated; despite they lead markets toward a more monopolistic, and less competitive environment (example: Careem's acquisition by UBER). While many entrepreneurs seek investment after stepping into the bandwagon, without realizing that in the USA less than 0.1% of ventures receive VC (as per a report on Forbes). One can imagine if the trend to seek venture funds is further ingrained in the minds of aspiring Pakistani entrepreneurs, the short supply of funds (let alone its possible corrupting influence) will do more harm than good in promoting the culture of entrepreneurship in the country. This trend has hijacked even the meaning of the term entrepreneurship, so much so that those who create ventures delivering superficial value to their users just to make an exit or getting hooked with a VC, are now only referred to as entrepreneurs. The influence of financial capital has shifted the focus of entrepreneurs from innovating for the end-users to innovating for the financial market only (see Tim O' Reilly's book 'What's the Future', and Jaron Lanier's 'Who Owns the Future' for details). This trend must not continue.

Entrepreneurs must create real value for real users. This perhaps is only possible if entrepreneurs keep a distance from the influence of financial markets. Staying away from the institutional investment is also beneficial for operational reasons as well as explained earlier. Growing organically while bootstrapping, and gradually increasing the complexity of the operations is perhaps the appropriate way. Innovative ideas emerge from the combination of real-time interaction with the customers, market intelligence, and intuition grounded in a real-time experience. But for that, one should already be operating in the market for a few years. It is perfectly alright to start a traditional business as the goal should be to establish oneself in the market with the available resources. Once a cash-cow has been developed, you have the luxury to experiment on an innovative idea.

But why innovate in the first place. If the goal is to attract more customers, then please note that winning customers in the Pakistani market can be best done through superior customer service, as Pakistani customers typically fancy respectful treatment. By making your customer feel special you can beat the competitors in almost every market domain. Interestingly, to make customers feel special, and give them due respect doesn't cost a dime. You just need to know how to talk respectfully and deliver a little more than you promise. Employees can be won likewise.

Innovation must only be pursued if an entrepreneur is genuinely interested in improving a certain aspect of customer experience or solving an unsolved problem in society. Carl Schramm argues that innovators are mission-oriented, and do not do it for money. They have an urge to create a better world by contributing their bit. They are rewarded nevertheless by customers for creating value. So to innovate, you must genuinely consider the wellbeing of your target audience as supreme, and your self-interest as secondary. That doesn't imply giving products or services for free. You can sell for a profit to ensure the sustainability of your venture, and improve your capacity to take your proposition to a wider audience.

Nassim Nicholas Talib argues that creating a genuine innovation takes years of customer or user feedback; often it takes decades of refinement which results in the creation of a better solution to a prevailing problem, more so if multiple entrepreneurs compete in the process. This is seldom possible while ensuring interest in financial markets for the reasons mentioned above. There are hidden costs or side effects behind innovations that sometimes surface after many years, like the influence of burning fossil fuels on the climate or impact of plastics on the food chain. These side effects or their costs eventually decide the future of innovation. However, if the interest of the financial market gets hooked with an insidious innovation, they try their level best to obscure the knowledge of side effects or suppress innovations. Genuinely beneficial innovations with no hidden costs therefore can come from competing entrepreneurs engaged with real customers under no influence of financial markets. That's the kind of entrepreneurial environment we need to produce in Pakistan.

Three Reasons Why Business Plans are Ineffective

Business Plan is a lengthy document that is prepared lots of brain muscle to work market gaps, competition dynamics, financial feasibility, expected profits, projected cash flow, tentative organizational structure, etc.

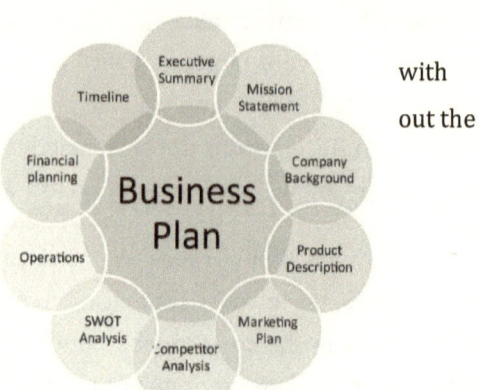

with out the

The purpose is to provide an economic justification for establishing a business to a potential venture

capitalist to invest in business ideas for possible returns in the future.

The major problem is that the effectiveness of this document is more hypothetical than real! and can cause trouble in the following ways if you are new in the business.

1. Future is unpredictable:

A Business plan is based on the idea that the future of the market can be predicted by looking at past trends. Welcome to the fool's paradise. The market is a dynamic, continuously evolving system. In today's world, the rate of change in market trend has only sped up thanks to the speed at which technology is transforming.

Even if you try to develop a business plan looking at the present conditions of the market, more especially consumer trends, the document might become obsolete during the weeks or months you spend preparing it. This might not be the case in the 1960s or 70s, however today it is, due to rapid changes occurring in consumer behavior. There is also a time lag, i.e. if there is a change inside the brains of your potential consumers, then you will know it only after a while which could be weeks, months particularly when it becomes visible as a trending behavior. Till the time you become aware, brains of your potential consumers could already have drifted elsewhere.[4]

Furthermore, if you are new in the business, it is very difficult to get an accurate legacy or record of consumer behavior which could be extrapolated into the future to make forecasts. Even if you get these the necessary data or insights, still there is no way to confirm the validity of future projection. This I have seen while working for a home appliance manufacturer, where despite tons of energy spent on forecasting future sales, the average forecasting accuracy never exceeded 20% despite the availability of all the necessary historical data.

---

[4] Image source: https://www.istockphoto.com

So here is your first catch, you are virtually blind, and instead of accepting it, you are pretending that you can see things going on inside the brains of your consumers! Predicting what would be inside their brains is even a bigger challenge. Even if you become successful in gathering a lot of data, through secondary, and even primary sources, it becomes really dangerous, as the data brings a false illusion with it! You enter into a hubris feeling that you now know with certainty, but in actuality, there is no way to be sure.

2. Planning something too big to manage

The Business plan is prepared by default to set up a complete business organization with all its functions fully operational. Often business plans do not explain how these individual functions would interact with each other, and what would be the structure of rules which would define the nature of their interdependent interaction. This approach completely ignores the idea that complex systems do not jump out of thin air, rather they gradually, and organically evolve in the marketplace over the years, and even decades. Now if you attempt to do it otherwise, and erect something big, and complex in the first go which is also far from your capacity to manage, then it is not too hard to understand that you might end up in a disaster. Instead, one may start with baby steps, and grow gradually

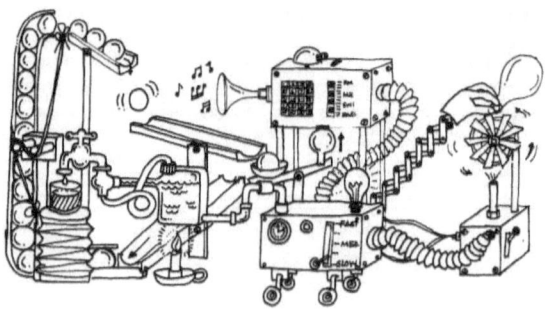

3. The Embedded Intellectual Arrogance

Another thing which contributes in the above problem is that a nice clean document prepared with lots of hard work, which contains lots of intricate graphs, and tables, flashy terms, and calculations, etc. would probably make you arrogant, and trap you into hubris while making it difficult to accept a mistake which you might
make during the practical implementation of your plan. Now, this is lethal. As during a business start-up particularly if you're doing it for the first time, you may expect yourself to make a lot of mistakes, and embrace lots of surprises ... but if you have already made up your mind regarding what to expect, and how to respond, then this rigidity may come with a price tag that you might not be able to afford.

The Alternative

Jim Collins notes in his book 'Built to Last', that all the organizations which he studied, don't rely on strategic planning, rather they "try a lot of stuff, and keep what's working"... As per Collin's observation, he found the Darwinian rule of "survival of the most adaptable" to be at work rather than complicated business strategies. Ricardo Semler, CEO of Semco Corporations, in his talk at MIT titled 'Leading by Omission', also argued on the same lines saying it's never really possible to predict, and there is too much gap between the forecasted figures and the actual. Furthermore, Nassim Nicholas Talib in his book 'The Black Swan' argued that despite how good the intelligence functions of the military might be; they never compromise on their ability to swiftly respond to any attack, and the same applies for business.

During the start-up, when nothing is certain, and you are inexperienced, the skill that can help you the most is your ability to quickly adapt, and respond to any new surprise that struck you anytime in the marketplace. Furthermore how afraid are you to make mistakes, and learn from them... if you are, then surely the business plan method would attract you more as its intellectual appeal tempts you to believe that there is indeed a way where things can go as predicted, also without compromising on the demands of your ego.

So how can we start a business without a business plan, we got to have some plan! Isn't it? Yes indeed, but not the type of a typical business plan which is taught in business schools. Part 2 of this book will walk you through the step by step process.

Chapter 4...

Some Myths about Starting a Business

Many new students often share these apprehensions about starting their own business or becoming an entrepreneur. They rather prefer to become an employee of an already existing business, preferably a large famous corporation. I would rather call these apprehensions as myths, as I have read, and seen myself in numerous business start-up experiences, here they are:

Myth 1: Lots of Capital is required

It is possible to start a business without or limited capital particularly if it's a service-related business. You might some to invest later on but not to initiate, or there are some ideas where capital investment is mandatory, but let us avoid such ideas if you are new in the game, as if you are not you probably do not need this book. More important than capital, and more important the business idea itself, you rather need connections with people who have capital or goods which you may need to sell to some potential customer., and of course, you need market knowledge, technical skills to understand the product, and necessary experience of dealing in the market you intend to launch a product. But most importantly, you should ask: do I know the right kind of people who can facilitate me in the process of launching my business. Look around, is there anyone in your family, friends, etc., who can provide you raw material, space to sell or any other

service on credit, or if there is a
potential customer in your friends or
family, who can pay you advance to
buy something they need?

If yes then you are through! You have
started a business without investing a
rupee of your own. Now this means you need to have lots of friends or a big
social circle, as more people you know (who also trust you, of course), the
more you have the chance of finding a supplier or a customer who can
cooperate with you in such a fashion.

So more important than capital are your contacts, as entrepreneurship is
simply a game of systemically, sustainably connecting people who would
benefit from their engagement with your start-up either financially or by
experiencing the benefit of the product or service you are offering. Now
once you have started the cycle of rolling cash, you can gradually reinvest
your profits, and expand your customer base... Remember your experience
with your previous customer, and their testimonial is your biggest selling
point. More on this later on.

Myth 2: Need some Job experience to start a business

Doing a job in a specific business function in an established business, and
starting a business scratch are two different things altogether. Read See
Michael Garber's 'E-Myth Revisited' for details. When you do a job, you
learn part of a process that is required to turn the wheel of a business
organization, not the whole of it. So often your technical expertise in a
specific business function only makes you believe that you can sell the

same expertise into the market, or use it to start the same business, which is rather a composite of lots of processes, and a variety of expertise.

Also according to Steve Blank, a start-up is not necessarily a miniature of a large corporation, often start-ups are established, and operated in a very different (chaotic) fashion in comparison to the business unit of a large corporation. This is so because nothing is structured within a start-up. So instead of job experience, what you need is:

- A lot of (un)common sense,
- Ability to coordinate between different business functions,
- Multitasking as you might have to do everything (selling, purchasing, accounting, etc.) yourself in the beginning,
- Lots of patience with lots of determination,
- Self-discipline, and ability to avoid over commitments, and the ability to fulfill commitments that you have made.

Often a job experience does help in this context, however, that experience has to be rich enough to cover all important business functions necessary for the startup. Maybe a sales-oriented job helps you to experience interaction with customers or suppliers … But not quite so if it's a typical office 9 to 5 job. Working in a small business where one gets exposure to every aspect of the value chain may help, however.

Another drawback is you getting used to the job environment, and when you advance in your career, your comfort zone established with the structured environment might become a psychological barrier in starting up your venture. Furthermore, as you grow old, your family responsibilities also multiply, hence your ability to take risks also reduces the addition of family members. If you are not feeling confident, then doing an internship for a few months in a small business, similar to the one you intend to start, may help. Having a mentor who can guide through different steps of the process may also be beneficial.

See Appendix 1 for more insights.

Myth 3: Doing business is riskier than doing a job

Yes unless it's a government job. But otherwise, the business which employs you can also fail ... if it does then eventually its employees (including you) suffer as well. One can argue that the risk of failure in  the start-up is very high. But there are ways to reduce risks explained in later sections of this book.

Furthermore, it's also too subjective to assume that chances of failure are greater for entrepreneurs than for employees, as you can also be kicked out of the job. Besides, there will be a huge psychological set back if you are fired from a job, even if it was not your fault. The dependency on regular paycheques can be lethal in this sense; but if you are an entrepreneur, accustomed to uncertainty, always mentally prepared for it, so if your business collapses, then you are in a relatively better psychological state than an unemployed person. In any case, a careful, no-nonsense, and intelligent entrepreneur wouldn't keep all his eggs in one basket and would diversify to the extent possible to minimize his risks.

And from an Islamic perspective, *Rizq* is determined by Allah s.w.t, so if whatever is written in your name will be provided to you if you made an honest effort for it. Interesting as an entrepreneur you experience this on an almost daily basis. So this concept makes lots of related apprehensions irrelevant for a Muslim entrepreneur. So concentrate on increasing *Barakah* in your *Rizq* by having faith in Allah's (s.w.t) mercy, and doing only the halal or legitimate things even if the profitability is seemingly less in doing so. Remember, according to a hadith 90% of a *Rizq* goes to traders, businessmen, and only 10% goes to the employed.

Myth 4: Need a very innovative idea

Why? As long as there is a valuable item in your hand, and that means almost everything, even garbage has some value for someone, you can sell it to the person who needs it. Don't look at some innovative ideas; rather find an opportunity to complete a chain between a supplier, YOU, and a customer, innovative ideas can come later, first  important thing is to get the cash flow cycle rolling. I am not suggesting that innovation is bad in the beginning, but it shouldn't get on to your nerves, and an excuse for not moving forward. On the other hand, for innovation to be really practical, first you need to spend some time studying the value chain of your business to understand the gaps, and the possibility of certain innovative ideas to fill those gaps. Before that, it's only a wild guess. Starting therefore is much more important than innovating.

These gaps can be anywhere in between the value chain, i.e. product design, packaging, distribution, payment method, sales method, customer service or relations, etc, but you can't notice unless you are in the market doing business yourself. Yes, you need to start the cycle of delivering the product/service to the customer, and receive payments, and to do that you don't need an idea which is out of this world. Start with selling vegetables for example, and see where are the gaps in the chain? You will surely see them in a few months if you have an eye for it ... How can you ever know how deep the rabbit hole goes unless you don't decide to go down, and see it yourself!

Chapter 5...

Some Broad Guidelines

If you want to start a business all that you need to do is to commercially connect three stakeholders (a) supplier/vendors, (b) yourself (or your team), and (c) customer (that's the first step, of course, employees will come later) ... so ask yourself (a) are there any supplier available within your easy reach of the product or its raw material who can give you supplies necessary on easy terms or perhaps on credit? (b) Are there customers of the same product available within your reach or of some of your contacts, who can also agree to pay an advance against your product or service in case the supply side such facility isn't available? (See the chapter on 'where to find a business idea' on page 85) If you have a big idea in your mind, consider scaling it down into something so simple that you can handle it with ease but outside of your comfort zone. For example, if you want to start a fast-food chain, start with a small french-fries or burger-cart which would not take more than Rs. 30,000 - 40,000 to establish. If you're feeling some shame, check how KFC and McDonalds started, or Shaan Foods or Sitara Textiles started. Dr. Amjad Saqib's book 'Kamyab Log' is full of such examples ...

OR If you intend to set up an industrial stitching unit, and export garments then start with a tailoring shop if your resources and experience limit you ... If you want to set up a factory of shoe manufacturing, this can be started with a small investment in the purchase of raw material only by outsourcing the production to already established small manufactures, while selling the shoes online. An entrepreneur is one who scales up a simple business model by creating a system to perform all business functions automatically like a synchronized machine. An entrepreneur is initially self-employed, as he or his team has to take care of all the operations themselves. However very soon they realize that various routine tasks can be simply dedicated to a specialized person. So they may write down the details of the processes to make work-flow-charts or Standard Operating Procedures (SOPs), and hire a person to hand over the routines. Gradually they may divide all the routine tasks being performed in all key functions like purchase, sales, production, accounts, marketing, operations, etc., and slowly create a structured organization by hiring individuals suitable for each set of functions. See the book E-Myth by Michael Garber for details.

Of course, there will be uncertainties, surprises, disappointments, etc., but that's part of the game, and that's exactly how we learn, but eventually, structure refines, and gradually business functions are taken up by employees.

Once this is done, entrepreneurs end up creating a system to manufacture a product or deliver a service to the customers. He is now relatively free to take up other challenges or think about scaling up, or start some new ventures, or whatever. This system is the real product of an entrepreneur, says Michael Garber, which also has a price tag, and can be sold to another party, if required. Once you have started a simple business, and have been able to successfully manage the flow of product in one direction (supplier to customer), and flow of cash in the other direction (customer to suppliers), you are now aware of the challenges, barriers, pitfalls, hurdles, etc. faced in the process, and how to go around them... this experience brings you an insight about the dynamics of the market and reveals any gaps which are required to be filled.

If you haven't been through this, and haven't jumped into the ocean, your evaluation can only be hypothetical and would lack any authentication or backed by experience ... therefore conventional gap analysis was done by Business School students, and subsequent development of a business and marketing plan around the gap might end up in disappointment, and loss ... This typical business school methodology also requires a considerable amount of market insight, and the ability to foresee how things would turn out to be in the market ... but the dilemma is, in a market place things change fast, and no one is sure what will happen next.

Therefore the ability to quickly respond to the rapidly changing environment is more important than the ability to foresee what's coming next ... at the end of the day what matters is how agile you are. Entrepreneurs who are not exactly entrepreneurs, but are self-employed with lots of helpers, cannot afford to be agile, entrepreneurs who have designed a system are not overburdened to react to the changing environment; they also design their systems to change accordingly.

To cut the story short, to be an entrepreneur the practical steps one needs to take can be summarized as follows:

1. Don't plan something too big that it's beyond your capacity to manage, even if it can be materialized somehow...

2. Reduce your idea into a small simple practical trade based model. Slowly move toward processing or production if required...

3. Change the model to the extent you can. Find supportive suppliers, and willing customers; hold back your passion for a while...

4. Experience managing the cycle of delivering the product, and accepting payments...

5. Find the gaps in the market you have stepped into already, and have tasted the bitterness...

6. Be agile...

7. Create a flexible system for routine operations...

8. Expand gradually by hiring employees...

9. Refine the system, smoothen the flow, sit back, and enjoy the show...

Chapter 6...

An Alternative Paradigm

For quite a while we have been exploring, and experimenting with an alternative methodology for a start-up for those who don't have many resources, and experiences to initiate with. Though the method can be used by anyone. The conventional method taught in MBA programs where involving a venture capitalist is necessary also has a spectacular failure rate of more than 75%[5], and according to some more than 90%[6] in their first 5 years of inception.

This desperately demands an alternative method as well for the newcomers who also can't afford to lose much. Besides the amazing failure rate of the conventional methodology itself is a good reason to find an alternative methodology. The following are some differentiating features for this alternative approach. Some of the organic approaches have already explained above, however here it is contrasted with the conventional method to see how different it is.

1. Idea centric vs. Resource centric

The conventional method requires the idea to be the next big thing! The revolutionary idea which would sweep the market, even if it is 10% of the next big thing, it is presented as if it is. Every business plan competition is

---

[5] See Steve Blank's HBR article 'Why The Lean Startup Changes Everything'
[6] See Michael Gerber's book 'E-Myth Revisited'

there to reinforce this very concept, where the biggest, most innovative idea is getting the top prize. This prerequisite demands the concerned to make lots of assumptions about the possible demand of the proposed proposition based on market conditions, and competitor information, etc., and then allocate costly strategies to capture that demand. Here comes the role of a venture capitalist or a banker who would finance the business. Even if you are successful in getting the millions necessary for the start-up, do you have enough experience to handle the entire thing? If you have then go-ahead, but if you are a beginner then obviously there is a problem! It's like diving in a deep-sea without learning how to swim! You would face lots of surprises, and challenges big enough to knock you down!

On the contrary, the alternative approach demands one to focus on say how much money one has at the beginning in his pocket, what skills one has, what resources are available in one's network which would be required at any stage of the supply chain (suppliers, buyers, vendors, etc.), are there any angel investors in the network, etc. Once all the resources are chalked down then one can work-out with all these known variables that what kind of a business is possible now! The most important resource is your network (family, relatives, friends, professional contacts, etc.) who can share their experience and resources with you. This is a bottom-up approach in contrast with the top-down conventional approach.

2. Lots of capital vs. Lots of contacts

It's a common misconception that lots of capital (millions if not billions) is needed to start a business, and if not available then eventually investment from a venture capitalist or borrowing from a bank is required. The idea is to invest millions to make millions in a niche market segment. The idea sometimes is to capture market share which is occupied by other direct or indirect competitors, in the context of 'Social Darwinism' (Herbert Spencer's, not Darwin's idea), where the fittest survives. To build muscles quickly you need steroids or lots of fast money to penetrate the market, but that has its side effects.

The experience suggests otherwise. Most medium-sized or small entrepreneurs say that you can start a business without capital, but you cannot start without having enough contacts. Pakistani society is peculiar in this context. The communities in Pakistan with stronger family bonds are more entrepreneurial than those which are not. Like Memon, Dehli Wala, Pathan, Dawoodi Bohra, Gujrati, Ismaili, or Chinioti communities (etc.) have a business-oriented culture, and the newcomers have all the support from within the respective communities in which they belong to. If you don't belong to such a community then still you need to expand your circle of friends and get well connected with your relatives, and neighbors as well. Darwin would agree that organisms (businesses, in the context above) with stronger communal ties have a better chance of survival and those which are most adaptable to change[7].

3. Advertising Expense vs. Word of Mouth

When the goal is to make hundreds of millions by investing millions in a product proposition which is new to the customers then it is little surprise that lots of money need to be spent on marketing of the product. The advertising expense is also built into the product cost hence raising its price. The method operates like a vicious circle while consuming lots of

---

[7] Jim Collins in his book 'Built to Last' (see where the author explains myth no. 8) has suggested that theories of Darwin has more relevance in explaining organizational behaviour in the market as compare to typical management theories

financial resources with little guarantee of success. Despite all the expenses on advertising, customer loyalty is more dependent on the product quality, and post-purchase facilitation rather than the glamour in the ads.

On the contrary, the above is unthinkable for a start-up with little budget. Some basic communication with potential buyers is necessary; however, it is important that in the beginning the focus should be on the product quality, and ensuring customer loyalty so that the satisfied customers generate word of mouth for you. If your product is generating word of mouth, and every happy customer is sending more customers than your product penetration will grow exponentially in a short time. Your product should become viral to be successful, period. If you start with only one customer and assume he or she brings in two more, and each of these two brings two more, then the rest is simple math. This is, of course, hypothetical, however in reality the curve would grow much faster perhaps, and within a few months, you may become unstoppable, only if your product or service satisfies the customer needs[8].

4. Fixed assets vs. working capital

The conventional approach insists on having a brand image to impress which would be built through a very nicely decorated office, and lots of employees, etc. Also when it talks about generating lots of sales volumes then a warehouse and a manufacturing setup (if it is required) becomes mandatory.

The alternative approach doesn't require any of this to start. You can start from right where you are standing or sitting right now. Since you are

---

[8] See HBR article 'The One Number You Need to Grow', URL: https://hbr.org/2003/12/the-one-number-you-need-to-grow

working within the people you know like your friends, relatives, etc. therefore you don't need to spend much to impress them. Furthermore, you are also not required to invest in heavy machinery unless it is extremely necessary, it is better to outsource any manufacturing process to any of your friends or family members (remember the bottom-up approach mentioned earlier). Much of your investment would go into working capital which would be recycled as soon as you sell off your inventory. This way, much of the risk can be avoided, and you can better focus on learning about the challenges in your replenishment cycle. Once you are through the learning phase and have built a network of buyers, now you can move toward acquiring fixed assets as per your business needs.

5. Foresightedness vs. Agility

According to Ricardo Semler (in one of his talks at MIT titled 'Leading by Omission') the conventional business plan method is the legacy of the military-industrial complex which dominated the industry during the world wars, where planning was based on intelligence reports. The trend has continued to date, and the MBA's way of starting a business requires the concerned to gather market data to identify profitable gaps, gather competitor information, and then accordingly design the product, and its pricing promotional, and placement strategy. This requires massive data-gathering exercises, and which can often cost hundreds of thousands of rupees. The philosophical justification of such a method comes from the objective of making tons of money in the shortest possible time, and that isn't possible unless a market segment with low competition and high demand is identified. But the problem is market intelligence reports are seldom accurate about market behavior or customer acceptance, also that the conditions in the market changes often rapidly, making the predictions or forecasting irrelevant.

The alternative method emphasizes more on response readiness! If marketing conditions change then one should be able to adapt and change according to the changing trends of the market. This isn't easy particularly when some venture capitalist has invested large sums in your business. The pressure of commitments with the VC would force concerns to remain inflexible hence often leading to failures.

6. Financial Dependence vs. Financial Independence

The large sums of money which are required to set up your business the MBA's way aren't often available with you. This means you have to meet some venture capitalists in most cases who would invest. This is rather like being an unpaid employee of the venture capitalist or bank till the time breakeven isn't achieved, and till the time the business isn't transformed into a cash cow. This doesn't happen in 75% of the cases as mentioned above, which means the fear of failure traumatizes the entire process of business development and rather becomes a crippling force that itself contributes to the failure of business start-up.

The Organic Alternative requires that you start with your pocket money or angel investment, and roll the sum of your investment many times over in a month to get you returns. This means you would start from a trade based model. In a service-oriented business, the only cost incurred is of advertising, and if you have a large network available then this is also negligible. You grow slowly by reinvesting your sums. This seems like a very slow process but it has a potential of exponential growth if you have been able to prepare the foundations well. There are many successful examples in Pakistan of this alternative approach.

7. Linear growth vs. Organic growth

When there are large investments involved, and the breakeven point is a few years down the line then the conventional method requires sustained growth for 5 - 10 years in the direction outlined by the business plan. What if there are new opportunities that emerge down the line? What if the preconceived ones begin to diminish on the way? What if market trends shift in some other direction? All of this makes the conventional method quite inflexible.

The organic model goes with the flow, as the opportunity arrives, you try to capitalize on it! But of course, you need to be financially independent to do so. You need to follow the path of least resistance. With a smaller team, and business size, you can do this, and that's exactly what you have in the beginning.

8. Risk-Taking vs. Risk Aversion

There is a common misconception that great entrepreneurs are risk-takers; there is a difference between risk-taking and gambling, and also there is a threshold of the risk which one can afford.

We need to calculate how much loss we can afford, a digestible amount would allow us to sleep at night in case we lose it. Also operating within your network of friends, and family allows you to start with people you already know therefore the fundamental most significant risk is reduced if not eliminated, that is, of dealing with new people, and trusting with them with payments, and supplies. Nature has a design for our growth; our experience grows incrementally over time as we take small steps forward. Giant leaps often lead to big falls leading to financial, and psychological loss big enough to leave a devastating blow which might cripple you for the rest of your life. One step at a time, one step at a time, one step at a time, moving forward in baby steps is the way to go. But no excuse for laziness, and lethargy...

9. Arrogance vs. Humility

Business schools pump arrogance in their MBAs. This might be necessary within a premise of cut-throat competition, where humility is rather seen as a weakness. Furthermore, the ideology within which this is justified idealizes individuals who are at the top of the hierarchy, are wealthy and independent in all aspects of their lives. Being arrogant over one's successes is therefore understandable (not justifiable). Those who aren't yet on the top would rather act like one just to impress others. As Henry Mintzberg said, "Confidence minus competence equals arrogance".

This mind-set is a killer for the entrepreneurial spirit which rather requires one to remain humble, as in the beginning, one has to do all things himself, learn from mistakes and accept failures while maintaining a good relationship with all partners, and stakeholders. Starting up a business is not about getting ahead as an individual, but collaborating with lots of people for everyone's benefit. Humility doesn't mean that one begins to compromise on his goals to make others happy... Jim Collins suggests (see his book Good to Great) that top corporate leaders also possess humility coupled with a super strong will to eventually get results. When successful they give credit to everyone around, and upon failures, they prefer to look in the mirror.

10. Financial Management vs. Relationship Management

MBAs are trained to look at their employees as mere numbers on a balance sheet. During normal circumstances, their attitude toward others might be normal, but when pressure mounts on the head then the true face becomes visible to others. For typical MBAs, the bottom line is the only important aspect of the business, and everything else is a means toward that end. Once anything becomes a barrier it needs to be removed ASAPAGE With such a mind-set the relationship with the team members is only artificial and cosmetic.

On the other hand, the team is an entrepreneur's greatest asset. The relationship building, and sustaining mindset has to prevail as it would even extend to the customers, and all stakeholders. The financials are important however one can financially survive only when he or she can establish an enduring relationship with all his stakeholders, and clients. To build trust, and repute with others, the significance of honoring commitments, and giving respect to all deserves no mention. Humility is the most important asset in this context, while an arrogant attitude is a big liability.

Part – 2

Eleven Routes to start a business

Eleven Routes to start a business

Before asking, how to start, you must first ask yourself, what do you have? (a) An idea? (b) A unique skill set? (c) Industry experience? (d) Industry contacts? and/or (e) Capital? Identify yourself in the table, and jump to the relevant page to find the route most suitable for you.

Routes	Have an Idea	You or your partner have a skillset	Relevant industry experience	Relevant industry contacts	Capital	Go to Page no.
Blank state	-	-	-	-	-	43
Investor Mindset	-	-	-	-	✓	45
Archimedes	✓	-	-	-	-	48
Technician	-	✓	-	-	-	51
(Wo)man on a mission	✓	-	-	-	✓	54
Tech-investor	-	✓	-	-	✓	56
Macgyver	✓	✓	-	-	-	59
Visionary-tech-investor	✓	✓	-	-	✓	62
Guru	✓	✓	✓	-	-	65
Connector	✓	✓	✓	✓	-	68
Entrepreneur	✓	✓	✓	✓	✓	71

1. The Blank State

Scenario

- Have an idea: **X**
- You or your partner possesses a unique skill set: **X**
- Have relevant industry experience: **X**
- Have relevant industry contacts: **X**
- Have capital: **X**

Strategy

If you do not have anything, doing brokerage may be a good idea. Use your network to find a supplier of a product, and potential customers, take the product, one at a time, and sell it to a potential customer. If the supplier trusts you, you may get credit, if the customer trusts you, then you may get an advance payment. Focus on one customer at a time.

You can also bridge buyers, and sellers for a commission from both sides, many people sell cars likewise.

Gradually you can increase your customer base by generating positive word of mouth which is a result of happy customers talking positively on your back. Creating a positive word of mouth through satisfied customers is the most cost-effective, and effective way to increase sales. To create a satisfied customer base, their requirements must be understood from their perspective. Understand the problem they are seeking a solution to, not the product or service they seek. Try to solve the problem and the product or service you may provide could just be a part of the solution. Guide the customer toward the real solution to their problem even if it does not benefit you financially. That's fundamental in gaining customer's trust and establishing your credibility, which will eventually generate positive word of mouth.

Advantage: No prior investment required, and by connecting the buyers, and sellers you can learn about the behavior of all stakeholders, you can gain product knowledge, and discover your abilities to become self-employed. This can be the first step toward bringing all ingredients necessary to start a business in the future. Keep saving money to invest in your future business. Exposure to real market scenarios can also lead you to some viable business ideas to build a sustainable business, as ideas generated without exposure are good only in theory.

Requirements: Good interpersonal skills, strong empathy, good selling skills, patience, and cool temperament.

2. The Investor's Mindset

Scenario

- Have an idea: **X**
- You or your partner possesses a unique skill set: **X**
- Have relevant industry experience: **X**
- Have relevant industry contacts: **X**
- Have capital: ✓

Strategy

Often people come up with their query that I have some money, what kind of a business I should start in this amount. This question is incorrect. Because there are far more important things than capital which an entrepreneur needs to consider while having a sufficient amount of capital is not a guarantee of anything.

Capital can be an enabler, but cannot ensure the success of your venture. Evidence suggests that the most important thing is not even a business idea, as it may change as you move forward in the process of setting up a venture.

The most important asset any wanta-preneur possesses is perhaps his/her network! Starting a business is never an isolated phenomenon, as it rather requires working with suppliers, vendors, or third-party contractors, employees, retailers, and most importantly customers.

Strong interpersonal skills for effective management of relationships with all the stakeholders is perhaps the most essential trait a wanta-preneuer can possess before starting a business.

If you do not have any prior entrepreneurial, and industry experience. Then there are no shortcuts. First, you will have to gain entrepreneurial experience in a specific market segment. A segment in which you have enough people to support you in case you collapse. While you are learning how to swim, you may want to be in the water with people who you can trust, and who will support you in case you begin to sink.

Make a list of people in your contact list working in different industries or market domains who might be willing to give you a helping hand. If you decide to go to the B2B market then you better know in advance any potential customer who will be willing to avail your services or purchase your product. If you don't know such a corporate customer personally, then you must ask others in your network to help you connect with one.

See which of your connections can become or can connect you with a potential supplier, vendor, and third-party contractor. Looking at the list of potential stakeholders, and potential customers, you may work out a possible business idea, that is, you may find out a specific customer need which you can fulfill with the aid of the suppliers, vendors, and third-party contractors in your network.

If you have some potential customers, and no potential suppliers or vendors, then expand your network to find suppliers or vendors who are willing to work with you, if you cannot find in your immediate network then explore the network of the people already in your network. See page 77 for more details.

Once you are connected with all the stakeholders and can deliver a product or service to a target audience in your network (See page 113 for more details on how to identify a target audience), focus on one customer at a time! Remember your goal is to gain experience in the market, customer behavior, and behavior of other stakeholders. Let growth happen slowly, and gradually, let happy customers bring more customers by generating positive word of mouth which is considered to be the best marketing strategy by business experts.

Now gradually build your customer base while reinvesting profits. Once you have enough confidence in your venture, you may now invest your capital to expand.

Hire people to help you only when you think you can't meet customer demand on your own! (See page 123 for more details of hiring strategies)

Before investing in, one must work out how much one can afford to lose. Contrary to general perception, entrepreneurs globally are not gamblers, they very carefully calculate the risks, and try to minimize them as much as possible.

Keep cash safe for rainy days, and do not spend on anything which does not help your business grow by any means.

Your first goal should be to develop a cash cow for yourself, a self-sustaining business. Once you can achieve this, now put the business on autopilot by developing systems (see page 136 for details) now you can experiment in new areas to further diversify your portfolio?

3. Archimedes

Scenario

- Have an idea: ✓
- You or your partner possesses a unique skill set: **X**
- Have relevant industry experience: **X**
- Have relevant industry contacts: **X**
- Have capital: **X**

Strategy

How did you come across this idea of yours? Do you perceive a market gap or you faced a personal challenge forcing you to think for a solution? If it is just your perception that a product or a solution to a problem as you conceived is needed, then the idea may be hypothetical and will require testing.

Developing a product that does not exist anywhere in the world is extremely rare, so it is entirely possible that what you want to build might already exist.

See if a similar product exists elsewhere in the, 99.9% chance is that it might already exist, investigate to find it (see page 88 to find out how to search for a supplier in an international market) if it does not exist then investigate what has stopped others from bringing the product in the market.

If a product exists, try to import it by borrowing money from family or friends (see page 90 to find out how to import), and become a distributor (see page 140) of that existing product addressing the same problem you want to address. Think of manufacturing only when you have developed a sound customer base.

If you want to build a unique product, first discuss the concept with potential users (at least 25), and if the feedback is positive then think of building a prototype yourself (see page 109 for details) if you don't have the necessary skill-set then better acquire that skill set, or get a partner who has the skills (see page 83 for details). If that requires investment, see if your family, friends, or any relative can invest.

If they cannot invest, then you will have to first develop a source of income, save money, and then use it to develop the first fully functional prototype.

It is entirely possible that to reach a point where you have sufficient resources (finance, network, skills, etc.) to materialize your idea, you might have to go via a completely different route as directed by the existing resources you have right now. Question is, are you passionate enough to go to such lengths for your idea?

Even if you gather resources to develop your prototype you still have to show it to the potential users again to get their feedback to further refine the product.

Then you will have to find people to partner with who can help you mass produce, and distribute the product to your target audience.

If it's a service, then find the necessary connections with potential customers to deliver the service. You might have to partner with someone who has the necessary connections and the skillset.

Further, if your service requires help from third-party contractors, then better search for them as well. Prior connection with all stakeholders is a must. Focus on ways to build credibility (see page 75 for details) with the potential stakeholders before you begin to work with them.

Once you are connected with all the stakeholders and can deliver a product or service to a target audience in your network (See page 113 for how to identify a target audience), focus on one customer at a time! Remember in the beginning your goal is to gain experience in the market, customer behavior, and behavior of other stakeholders. Let growth happen slowly, and gradually, let happy customers bring more customers by generating positive word of mouth which is considered to be the best marketing strategy by business experts.

Now gradually build your customer base while reinvesting profits. Once you have enough confidence in your venture, you may now invest your capital to expand.

Hire people to help you only when you think you can't meet customer demand on your own! (See page 123 for more details of hiring strategies).

4. The Technician

Scenario

- Have an idea: X
- You or your partner possesses a unique skill set : ✓
- Have relevant industry experience: X
- Have relevant industry contacts: X
- Have capital: X

Strategy

If you are skilled, like if you are an engineer; think of a problem that exists in a society that can be addressed through your skillset.

Once you have figured out a problem, work out a practical solution that can be delivered at a price that the target audience can afford. But before that, it's important to shortlist a problem to work on.

Make a list of the problems that exist in society. Interview some wise people to help you refine that list. Research how these problems are being addressed globally.

Pick a problem whose solution you can work out keeping in view the skill set you, and your partner has, and the resources you both may possess.

Once a genuine workable problem is identified, see the simplest possible solution to it, while using no or least amount of technology. Imagine if technology can improve the solution, will the customer pay for it? How much they will pay (see page 121 for details).

Build a prototype yourself (see page 109 for details). If that requires investment, then see if your family, friends, or any relative can invest. If not then you will have to first develop a source of income, save money, and use it to develop the prototype (see page 109 for details). Question is, are you passionate enough to go to such lengths for your idea?

If you can build a fully functional prototype, show it to potential users who can give you brutally honest comments to improve. Remember, sometimes it can take many months to refine a product to marketable levels. It's manufacturing at a reasonable price, then it's selling, developing a system of customer support, is an entirely different ball game.

Alternatively, see if a similar product exists elsewhere in the, 99.9% chance is that it might already exist, investigate to find it (see page 88 to find out how to search for a supplier in an international market) if it does not exist then what have stopped others from bringing the product in the market.

- If a product exists, try to import it (see page 90 to find out how to import), and become a distributor (see page 140) of that existing product addressing the same problem you want to address. Think of manufacturing only when you have developed a sound customer base.
- If it's a service, then find the necessary connections with potential customers to deliver the service. You might have to partner with someone who has the necessary connections.
- Further, if your service requires help from third-party contractors, then better search for them as well. A prior connection with all stakeholders is a must. Focus on ways to build credibility (see page 75) with the potential stakeholders before you begin to work with them.

- If your proposition needs refinement, then you must engage with some potential customers to give you feedback on your offering. (See page 111 for details).

Once you are connected with all the stakeholders and can deliver a product or service to a target audience in your network (See page 113 for to know how to find your target audience), focus on one customer at a time! Remember in the beginning your goal is to gain experience in the market, customer behavior, and behavior of other stakeholders. Let growth happen slowly, and gradually, let happy customers bring more customers by generating positive word of mouth which is considered to be the best marketing strategy by business experts.

Now gradually build your customer base while reinvesting profits.

Hire people to help you only when you think you can't meet customer demand on your own! (See page 123 for more details of hiring strategies).

5. The (Wo)man on a Mission

Scenario

- Have an idea: ✔
- You or your partner possesses a unique skill set: **X**
- Have relevant industry experience: **X**
- Have relevant industry contacts: **X**
- Have capital: ✔

Strategy

Only having an idea, and capital to invest sounds more like a recipe for disaster. Being fixated on an idea, and relying solely on capital is one of the causes behind business failures. If you are passionate about your idea then you may want to test it first. Invite at least 25 potential users to critically comment on the idea. Take their feedback, and see if the idea survives.

The next step is to partner with someone who can help you build a prototype (see page 109 for details), and do pilot testing! As delivering any type of product or service needs a skilled person, even if the product is food one needs a chef to prepare.

Take feedback from potential users during pilot testing to further refine the product or service. Now work out who will be your supplier or third party contractor, who will be your customer particularly when it's a B2B product then If you decide to go in the B2B market you better know in advance any potential customer who will be willing to avail your services or purchase your product. If you don't know such a corporate customer personally, then you must ask others in your network to help you connect with one.

Having prior relationships with suppliers, vendors, or third-party contractors is helpful. If you do not know one, then use your network to find one, and approach through referrals. Randomly contacting any stakeholder will have credibility issues.

Use your capital only when extremely necessary. But before that work out how much you can afford to lose in case if the idea doesn't flourish. Contrary to general perception, entrepreneurs globally are not gamblers, they very carefully calculate the risks, and try to minimize them as much as possible. Keep your cash safe for rainy days, and leverage the resources in your network to build your business.

Once you are connected with all the stakeholders and can deliver a product or service to a target audience in your network (See page 113 to know how to identify your target audience), focus on one customer at a time! Remember your goal is to gain experience in the market, customer behavior, and behavior of other stakeholders.

Important thing is to satisfy customers, the quality of service is more important than quantity. Every happy customer brings more customers through word of mouth, which is considered the most effective marketing technique by business experts. Now gradually build your customer base while reinvesting profits. Generate sales, and try to achieve break-even as quickly as possible.

Hire people to help you only when you think you can't meet customer demand on your own! (See page 123 for more details of hiring strategies)

6. The Tech-Investor

Scenario

- Have an idea: **X**
- You or your partner possesses a unique skill set : ✓
- Have relevant industry experience: **X**
- Have relevant industry contacts: **X**
- Have capital: ✓

Strategy

If you are skilled, like if you are an engineer; think of a problem that exists in a society that can be addressed through your skillset. Once you have figured out a problem, work out a practical solution that can be delivered at a price that the target audience can afford. But before that, it's important to shortlist a problem to work on.

Make a list of the problems that exist in society. Interview some wise people to help you refine that list. Research how these problems are being addressed globally. Pick a problem whose solution you can work out keeping in view the skill set you, and your partner has, and the resources you both may possess.

Once a genuine workable problem is identified, see the simplest possible solution to it, while using zero or limited amount of technology. Imagine if technology can improve the solution then will the customer pay for it? (see page 121 for details)

Build a prototype yourself (see page 109 for details). If you can build a fully functional prototype, show it to potential users who can give you brutally honest comments to improve. Remember, sometimes it can take months to refine a product to marketable levels. It's manufacturing at a reasonable price, then it's selling, developing a system of customer support, is an entirely different ball game.

Before investing in any amount, one must work out how much one can afford to lose. Contrary to general perception, entrepreneurs globally are not gamblers, they very carefully calculate the risks, and try to minimize them as much as possible. You must try to save as much money as possible for rainy days.

Alternatively, see if a similar product exists elsewhere in the, 99.9% chance is that it might already exist, investigate to find it (see page 88 to find out how to search for a supplier in an international market) if it does not exist then investigate what have stopped others from bringing the product in the market.

- If a product exists, try to import it (see page 90 to find out how to import), and become a distributor (see page 140) of that existing product addressing the same problem you want to address. Think of manufacturing only when you have developed a sound customer base.
- If it's a service, then find the necessary connections with potential customers to deliver the service. You might have to partner with someone who has the necessary connections.
- Further, if your service requires help from third-party contractors, then better search for them as well. A prior connection with all stakeholders is a must. Focus on ways to build credibility (see page 75) with the potential stakeholders before you begin to work with them.

- If your proposition needs refinement, then you must engage with some potential customers to give you feedback on your offering (See page 111 for details).

Your first goal should be to develop a cash cow for yourself, a self-sustaining business. Once you can achieve this, now you may want to put the business on autopilot by developing systems (see page 136 for details) now you can experiment in new areas to further diversify your portfolio?

Once you are connected with all the stakeholders and can deliver a product or service to a target audience in your network, focus on one customer at a time! Remember your goal is to gain experience in the market, customer behavior, and behavior of other stakeholders. Let growth happen slowly, and gradually, let happy customers bring more customers by generating positive word of mouth which is considered to be the best marketing strategy by business experts. Now gradually build your customer base while reinvesting profits.

Hire people to help you only when you think you can't meet customer demand on your own! (See page 123 for more details of hiring strategies).

7. The MacGyver

Scenario

- Have an idea: ✓
- You or your partner possesses a unique skill set : ✓
- Have relevant industry experience: **X**
- Have relevant industry contacts: **X**
- Have capital: **X**

Strategy

How did you come across this idea? Do you want to build a product because you have the skill to do it or have you perceived a market gap, or you faced a personal challenge forcing you to think for an idea? If it is just your perception that a product or a solution to a problem as you conceived is needed, then the idea may be hypothetical and will require testing. Engineers, more than often, fall in the trap of making a product which they cannot make because it is needed by a market segment of potential buyers. Their emotional attachment with their creation often blinds them to see the uselessness of their product. So a genuine need in the society must exist which your invention can address. Discuss your idea with potential users, in the most self-critical manner possible (see page 111 for details)

Once a genuine need is identified, see the simplest possible solution to it, while using no or least amount of technology. Imagine if technology can improve the solution then will the customer pay for the price in exchange? (See page 121 for details)

Build a prototype yourself (see page 109 for details). If that requires investment, then see if your family, friends, or any relative can invest. If not then you will have to first develop a source of income, save money, and use it to develop the prototype. Question is, are you passionate enough to go to such lengths for your idea?

- If you can build a fully functional prototype, show it to potential users who can give you brutally honest comments to improve. Remember, sometimes it can take months to refine a product to marketable levels. It's manufacturing at a reasonable price, then it's selling, developing a system of customer support, is an entirely different ball game.
- See if a similar product exists elsewhere in the, 99.9% chance is that it might already exist, investigate to find it (see page 88 to find out how to search for a supplier in an international market) if it does not exist then what has stopped others from bringing the product in the market.
- If a product exists, try to import it (see page 90 to find out how to import), and become a distributor (see page 140) of that existing product addressing the same problem you want to address. Think of manufacturing only when you have developed a sound customer base.
- If it's a service, then find the necessary connections with potential customers to deliver the service. You might have to partner with someone who has the necessary connections.
- Further, if your service requires help from third-party contractors, then better search for them as well. A prior connection with all stakeholders is a must. Focus on ways to build credibility (see page 75) with the potential stakeholders before you begin to work with them.
- If your proposition needs refinement, then you must engage with some potential customers to learn direct feedback on your offering (see page 111 for more details).

Once you are connected with all the stakeholders and can deliver a product or service to a target audience in your network (See page 113 for more details), focus on one customer at a time! Remember your goal is to gain experience in the market, customer behavior, and behavior of other stakeholders. Let growth happen slowly, and gradually, let happy customers bring more customers by generating positive word of mouth which is considered to be the best marketing strategy by business experts. Now gradually build your customer base while reinvesting profits.

Hire people to help you only when you think you can't meet customer demand on your own! (see page 123 for more details of hiring strategies).

8. The Visionary Tech-Investor

Scenario

- Have an idea: ✓
- You or your partner possesses a unique skill set: ✓
- Have relevant industry experience: **X**
- Have relevant industry contacts: **X**
- Have capital: ✓

Strategy

How did you come across this idea? Do you want to build a product because you have the skill to do it or have you perceived a market gap, or you faced a personal challenge forcing you to think for an idea? If it is just your perception that a product or a solution to a problem as you conceived is needed, then the idea may be hypothetical and will require testing. Engineers, more than often, fall in the trap of making a product which they can not make because it is needed by a market segment of potential buyers. Their emotional attachment with their creation often blinds them to see the uselessness of their product. So a genuine need in society must exist which your invention can address. Discuss your idea with potential users, in the most self-critical manner possible (see page 113 for details)

Once a genuine need is identified, see the simplest possible solution to it, while using no or least amount of technology. Imagine if technology can improve the solution then will the customer pay for the price in exchange? (see page 121 for details).

Build a fully functional prototype (see page 109 for details), and show it to potential users who can give you brutally honest comments to improve. Remember, sometimes it can take years to refine a product to marketable levels. It's manufacturing at a reasonable price, then it's selling, developing a system of customer support, is an entirely different ball game.

See if a similar product exists elsewhere in the, 99.9% chance is that it might already exist, investigate to find it (see page 88 to find out how to search for a supplier in an international market) if it does not exist then what has stopped others from bringing the product in the market.

- If a product exists, try to import it (see page 90 to find out how to import), and become a distributor (see page 140) of that existing product addressing the same problem you want to address. Think of manufacturing only when you have developed a sound customer base.
- If it's a service, then find the necessary connections with potential customers to deliver the service. You might have to partner with someone who has the necessary connections.
- Further, if your service requires help from third-party contractors, then better search for them as well. A prior connection with all stakeholders is a must. Focus on ways to build credibility (see page 75) with the potential stakeholders before you begin to work with them.

Once you are connected with all the stakeholders and can deliver a product or service to a target audience in your network (See page 113 for more details), focus on one customer at a time! Remember your goal is to gain experience in the market, customer behavior, and behavior of other stakeholders. Let growth happen slowly, and gradually, let happy customers bring more customers by generating positive word of mouth which is considered to be the best marketing strategy by business experts. Now gradually build your customer base while reinvesting profits. Hire people to help you only when you think you can't meet customer demand on your own! (See page 123 for more details of hiring strategies)

Keep much of the cash safe for rainy days, and do not spend on anything which does not help your business grow by any means. Before investing in, one must work out how much one can afford to lose. Contrary to general perception, entrepreneurs globally are not gamblers, they very carefully calculate the risks, and try to minimize them as much as possible.

Your first goal should be to develop a cash cow for yourself, a self-sustaining business. Once you can achieve this, now evaluate if you want to put your business on autopilot or not (see page 123 for a detailed discussion) now you can experiment in new areas to further diversify your portfolio.

9. The Guru

Scenario

- Have an idea: ✔
- You or your partner possesses a unique skill set : ✔
- Have relevant industry experience: ✔
- Have relevant industry contacts: **X**
- Have capital: **X**

Strategy

Did your industry experience lead you to the identification of a problem, and to conceive a product/service to cater to that problem? If not then it means you are venturing into an area where you do not have necessary industry experience.

If yes, and if your skillset allows you to create a product to fill the identified gap then go for it. If it's a service, then find the necessary connections with potential customers to deliver the service. You might have to partner with someone who has the necessary connections.

Further, if your service requires help from third-party contractors, then better search for them as well. A prior connection with all stakeholders is a must. Focus on ways to build credibility (see page 75) with the potential stakeholders before you begin to work with them.

If your proposition needs refinement, then you must engage with some potential customer to give you feedback on your offering (see page 111 for details)

If it's a tangible product then still you have to go through the prototyping, and pilot testing process.

But first, see the simplest possible solution to the problem you have identified, while using no or least amount of technology. Imagine if technology can improve the solution then will the customer pay for the price in exchange? (See page 121 for details).

Build a prototype yourself (see page 109 for details). If that requires investment, then see if your family, friends, or any relative can invest. If not then you will have to use the personal savings to develop the prototype. It's very unlikely that any institutional investor like a venture capitalist would jump in to finance your R&D process. Consider finding an angle investor instead (see page 118 for a discussion regarding engaging angel investors)

If you can build a fully functional prototype, show it to potential users who can give you brutally honest comments to improve. Remember, sometimes it can take years to refine a technological product to marketable levels. It's manufacturing at a reasonable price (see page 121), then it's selling, developing a system of customer support (see page 129), is an entirely different ball game. If the product is already available in the market then setting up a manufacturing setup can be easier, but selling would be difficult due to competition (see page 145 for how to sell in the B2C market and page 148 for how to sell in B2B market).

See if a similar product exists elsewhere in the, 99.9% chance is that it might already exist, investigate to find it (see page 88 to find out how to search for a supplier in an international market) if it does not exist then what has stopped others from bringing the product in the market.

- If a product exists, try to import (see page 90 to find out how to import) or procure it from a local source, and become a distributor (see page 140) of that existing product addressing the same problem you want to address. Think of manufacturing only when you have enough customers to justify the investment.
- If it's a service, then find the necessary connections with potential customers to deliver the service. You might have to partner with someone who has the necessary connections.
- Further, if your service requires help from third-party contractors, then better search for them as well. A prior connection with all stakeholders is a must. Focus on ways to build credibility (see page 75) with the potential stakeholders before you begin to work with them.
- If your proposition needs refinement, then you must engage with some potential customers to give you feedback on your offering (see page 111 for details).

Once you are connected with all the stakeholders and can deliver a product or service to a target audience in your network (See page 113 for more details), focus on one customer at a time! Remember your goal is to gain experience in the market, customer behavior, and behavior of other stakeholders. Let growth happen slowly, and gradually, let happy customers bring more customers by generating positive word of mouth which is considered to be the best marketing strategy by business experts. Now gradually build your customer base while reinvesting profits. Hire people to help you only when you think you can't meet customer demand on your own! (See page 123 for more details of hiring strategies)

10. The Connector

Scenario

- Have an idea: ✓
- You or your partner possesses a unique skill set : ✓
- Have relevant industry experience: ✓
- Have relevant industry contacts: ✓
- Have capital: **X**

Strategy

Which approach did you use to work out the business idea? Is it causation or effectuation? In causation, you start by identifying a problem or market gap then see what resources will be needed to address that market gap, while in effectuation, you look at your skills, experience, contacts, and then see what market need can be addressed with what you already have. Former is recommended as entrepreneurs usually use it in contrast to a causal approach.

In effectuation, you ask yourself what type of business my means (skills, contacts, experience) allows me to start. In the light of the answer you set a goal, and then consult the contacts that can help you in setting a business, take their feedback, and evolve your proposition. The customers are also from within your contacts, so are the suppliers, vendors, or any third-party contractors.

So your focus is to find a synergy between all stakeholders, satisfy a particular customer need which you can satisfy with the help of the suppliers, vendors, or third-party contractors in your network. It's an iterative process as in the process of meeting your customer demands you will discover new opportunities, and will eventually find a way.

It's like constructing a big jigsaw puzzle when you don't know how the final picture will look, also when each puzzle piece keeps changing itself as well.

Lack of capital can be a barrier, and strength as well. Opportunity because it forces you to think more creatively, and leverage the resources existing in your network. You eventually realize that your credibility with stakeholders is your greatest asset which needs to be strengthened as you proceed ...

Do not think of investing in fixed assets, if manufacturing needs to be done, try outsourcing, at every step which would require capital investment, one must find creative ways to leverage the resources in one's networks to get the job done.

It takes a while (one or two years, sometimes three) to reach a point where you settle down with a portfolio of products with a continuous stream of revenues.

- If it's a service, then identify potential customers to deliver the service. If you cannot find partners in your immediate network, you might have to partner with someone who has the necessary connections (see page 83 for details).
- Further, if your service requires help from third-party contractors, then better search for them as well. A prior connection with all stakeholders is a must. Focus on ways to build credibility (see page 75) with the potential stakeholders before you begin to work with them.

- If your proposition needs refinement, then you must engage with some potential customer to give you feedback on your offering (see page 111 for details)

Once you are connected with all the stakeholders and can deliver a product or service to a target audience in your network (See page 113 on how to identify a target audience), focus on one customer at a time! Remember your goal is to gain experience in the market, customer behavior, and behavior of other stakeholders. Let growth happen slowly, and gradually, let happy customers bring more customers by generating positive word of mouth which is considered to be the best marketing strategy by business experts. Now gradually build your customer base while reinvesting profits.

Hire people to help you only when you think you can't meet customer demand on your own! (See page 123 for more details of hiring strategies).

11. The Entrepreneur

Scenario

- Have an idea: ✔
- You or your partner possesses a unique skill set : ✔
- Have relevant industry experience: ✔
- Have relevant industry contacts: ✔
- Have capital: ✔

Strategy

Which approach did you use to work out the business idea? Is it causation or effectuation? In causation, you start by identifying a problem or market gap then see what resources will be needed to address that market gap, while in effectuation, you look at your skills, experience, contacts, and capital, and then see what market need can be addressed with what you already have. Former is recommended as entrepreneurs usually use it in contrast to the causal approach.

In effectuation, you ask yourself what type of business my means (skills, contacts, experience) allows me to start. In the light of the answer you set a goal, and then consult your contacts who can help you in setting a business, take their feedback, and evolve your proposition. The customers are also from within your contacts, so are the suppliers, vendors, or any third-party contractors.

So your focus is to find a synergy between all stakeholders, satisfy a particular customer need which you can satisfy with the help of the suppliers, vendors, or third-party contractors in your network. It's an iterative process as in the process of meeting your customer demands you will discover new opportunities, and will eventually find a way.

It's like constructing a big jigsaw puzzle when you don't know how the final picture will look, also when each puzzle piece keeps changing itself as well ...

Having sufficient capital can be a barrier, and strength as well. Barrier because it often restricts you to think more creatively, and not force you to leverage the resources existing in your network. One must always remember that one's credibility with stakeholders is the greatest asset that needs to be strengthened with time ...

Know your affordable loss, and only invest that which you can afford to lose (if you lose the amount you will comfortably sleep at night). Contrary to general perception, entrepreneurs globally are not gamblers, they very carefully calculate the risks, and try to minimize them as much as possible.

Now see where it can be invested, ask yourself which of the resources I must possess without which it would be really difficult to satisfy my customers or expand my customer base. Office space is a good instrument to build credibility with the customers, so consider renting a decent place if necessary.

Do not jump toward investing in fixed assets unless extremely necessary, if manufacturing needs to be done prefer outsourcing; find creative ways to leverage the resources in one's networks to get the job done. Use your cash as little as possible, and save it for rainy days! Prepare for the time when you will have to pay salaries to your employees, and business would be going in a loss!

It takes a while (one or two years, sometimes three) to reach a point where you settle down with a portfolio of products with a continuous stream of revenues.

If it's a service, then identify potential customers to deliver the service. If you cannot find partners in your immediate network, you might have to partner with someone who has the necessary connections (see page 77 for details).

Further, if your service requires help from third-party contractors, then better search for them as well. A prior connection with all stakeholders is a must. Focus on ways to build credibility (see page 75) with the potential stakeholders before you begin to work with them.

If your proposition needs refinement, then you must engage with some potential customer to give you feedback on your offering (see page 111 for details)

Once you are connected with all the stakeholders and can deliver a product or service to a target audience in your network (See page 113 for details on how to identify a target audience), focus on one customer at a time! Remember your goal is to gain experience in the market, customer behavior, and behavior of other stakeholders. Let growth happen slowly, and gradually, let happy customers bring more customers by generating positive word of mouth which is considered to be the best marketing strategy by business experts. Now gradually build your customer base while reinvesting profits.

Hire people to help you only when you think you can't meet customer demand on your own! (See page 123 for more details of hiring strategies)

Part – 3

How to do stuff, some detail

1. How to build credibility?

Credibility is built when a person honors his words so many times that people with whom he or she committed begin to trust his words. This does not mean honoring commitments a hundred percent of the time, which is humanly impossible as there are so many things happening around us that are beyond our control. What is important is the effort that we make under difficult circumstances to honor our commitments, and when it becomes impossible for us then how do we compensate. Disappearing after committing is not the way. On the contrary, if it seems like that any part of the commitment is not possible to be kept, then do we inform the party beforehand about the causes, and what we are trying to do about it., and in case if we have to back off then how we are compensating for our inability to fulfill a commitment., and if our falling behind has incurred some loss on the party then how we are attempting to compensate for that loss. At the end of the day what matters is how serious we have been about the interest of the party with whom we have made the commitment, and how we demonstrate that seriousness with honest intent.

Self-awareness or the awareness of our ability to fulfill a commitment also matters as it is easy for people to overcommit without much consideration if they can fulfill the commitment or not. Often we are already occupied and accept a new job. This is not an issue of ill-intention, rather our inability to accept our limitations. So The question we need to ask ourselves is, are we honest without our selves, are we mindful of our limitations, are we considering a buffer for contingencies. A common example of a buffer is to ask for some extra time even if you know it will take like 5 days to complete a job, but still, you ask for 7 days just in case if there are contingencies. Also if surprises are common in your line of business, then are you honest about them with your stakeholder before committing? So in a nutshell, (a) honesty with oneself, and with stakeholder, (b) clear intentions, and (c) seriousness, and (d) consistent demonstration of these three qualities subsequently build credibility over time.

2. How to expand your network

One of the ways to develop new connections is when you are up to something, and you cannot get things done on your own. Now you need to get someone else involved but this someone you need is not in your existing network, you ask people for referrals, and some of your friends, relatives, neighbors, parents, siblings, etc. tell you that go, and talk to this person with my reference., and then you go, meet the person, and both of you find each other useful. Now you engage with the person, say a supplier, or a vendor, or a venue provider, or a mentor, or a customer, and both of you make some commitments like you commit paying an amount in exchange of a service or some supplies, or some venue, or whatever, when both parties honor their commitments, trust is developed, which is strengthened when both parties keep honoring their commitments.

Another way is when two people discover that they share an interest, and they begin to interact in a school, social media, or a conference, or a workshop, any social event, and begin interacting with each other, sharing stuff in which both are interested. This could be ideas, information, aspirations, concerns, pains, etc. However, this may not imply the person can be trusted in the time of need. For example, if you need money, will this fellow help you out? He or she would think, what if I lend him money, and he or she won't pay me back? I once needed a laptop but couldn't afford one due to my financial condition! One of my friends gave it to me for free. I also needed a place to work, but could not afford a space, a friend of a friend gave me a desk, and an internet connection to work in his office. I did not know the person at that time, but he trusted me because we had a mutual friend in between. This fellow is still my friend, and we both try to support each other as, and when needed. So you might connect with a lot of people through social media, however, I can tell by experience that you only discover who your true friends are only when you face a crisis in your life, or face a vulnerable situation, or are passing through rainy days.

The number of friend requests, and followers on social media increases when some of my posts get viral or is shared by a person who is already connected to lots of people. However, the real test of the connection happens when you ask for something, and the person in your contact doesn't disappoint you, and of course vice versa.

So in short, a connection has to be mutually beneficial, reciprocity is the name of the game! and if you are a man on a mission, then over time, you would meet new people, and the existence of mutual interest, reciprocity, the trust will allow the relationship to develop and sustain.

Mis-commitments, dishonesty, selfishness, manipulative behavior, abuse of power, etc. from any side cannot foster healthy relationships let alone sustain them.

The network is the topmost resource an entrepreneur possesses. This is my observation, and the opinion of various entrepreneurs I have interacted with. This is because setting up a business can never be a solo activity. Two stakeholders are fundamentally essential to your start-up, as emphasized earlier as well. (1) The supplier, and the (2) Customer. If you don't have the two in your contact list then the first thing you do is to look for them in your friends, family, neighbors, relatives, etc. contact lists. Ideally having a supplier or a vendor who could trust you with the supplies, and allows you to pay back later is the biggest advantage one can have. On the other hand, having a customer who can trust you with his money, and pays you in advance to receive the product later, is another great blessing. Much has already been written in this context. In this chapter, our focus would be to talk about how one can increase his network, and trust within the existing network.

Building a network is about building relationships. Let's start with the question, what is a relationship? The relationship is a bond between two individuals where both the individuals are benefiting from each other in a certain way. For example in a mentor, and an apprentice relationship, the apprentice is there to gain from the experience, and wisdom of the mentor, while the mentor earns the satisfaction of contributing positively in the life of his student. The benefit is not supposed to be monetary all the time, there are various sorts of non-monetary, and qualitative types of gains one could experience from all around! What does a parent gain when he or she spends leisure time with his or her kids? The answer can only be known by the parents who understand the happiness when they see their children's faces glittering with joy. What does a relief-work volunteer gain after taking the pain of traveling thousands of miles to a disaster struck area to help the ones devastated by a certain natural calamity? It's nothing materialistic of course.

The purpose of all these examples is to set the context that the exchange which happens between two individuals to form a lasting relationship doesn't have to be quantitative, and financial at all. People are attracted to you when you have something to offer, like respect, concern, care, empathy, passion to contribute, etc., and all of these things come directly from inside you! and you don't have to be rich to offer all of these.

But one needs to be careful. There are two kinds of people around you! 1) Those who want to take advantage of you or exploit you when you are nice with them, and 2) those who acknowledge your contribution, and want to return you the favor when you do good to them. As per my experience, most of the people I have ever met fall in the category of Type-2, whereas Type-1 is out there but their behavior is mostly conditioned by certain negative experiences in their past. You however need to become a good judge of character so that you don't mistakenly put your trust in the wrong type. This is learned through experience, or probably the hard way! Having a mentor might help as well.

Entrepreneurs need to keep such points in their minds, as their efforts are collaborative! If you already don't have someone in your network who can help you complete the cash flow cycle (from supplier to the buyer), then you can connect with people that would get you through! You may ask yourself: Am I a passionate individual, with a strong character, a disciplined attitude, and shows genuine respect without flattering, if yes then you will find the right person within the network of your network ... if not in your network.

We don't generally connect with people without a referral, this might also happen, however mostly you should find a referral who could connect you with the right person. This would substantially reduce the ice-breaking phase. For this purpose, it's a great idea to be in the good books of certain people who are very well connected to lots of people. Like presidents of various associations for example. So instead of going directly, you might ask the well-connected fellow to introduce you with the right person.

Another important aspect of networking is being clear with your values. When two individuals who agree on certain values meet each other for the first time, it doesn't take much time to connect. However on the other hand when the values don't match, matchmaking isn't much possible. You might ask if someone has something you need, but he or she believes in some other types of values (vulgarity, showoff, etc.), and you might have to compromise on your values, to reach to them, then my dear friend, you need to ask, where your values yours in the first place as you prefer to compromise them for some short term benefit? Remember your integrity standing on the strength of character is one of your strongest assets! Losing it would mean losing everything you have accumulated over the years unless you are a celebrity for whom any kind of publicity negative or positive would increase in his or her fame...

I have an introverted personality, and in a networking event connecting with someone whom I don't know is the last thing on my mind. However, if I feel interacting with a certain individual will help me advance my passion in a certain way, then I find the courage to do so. Recently I went to a conference in Doha, where I asked questions to the speakers to make myself noticed to various notable scholars. Being a part of such events in any capacity brings you lots of opportunities to interact with lots of people, and subsequently stumbling upon certain people with mutual interest.

Remember it's a very long term, iterative, and continuous process! Having a short term, self-centered approach, and impatience can be counterproductive. If you perceive a contact as a means to an objective higher than your selfish-materialistic-interest, then the possibility of a strong connection might increase substantially. You cannot make friends for the sake of making friends but in the process of achieving a higher cause.

But isn't entrepreneurship is about making money! It is, and it isn't! Any successful entrepreneur would admit that money comes when you put the benefit of others before your self-interest. It is like karma at work, primarily you have to think about benefiting or helping your customers at large, and they in return become loyal and generate positive word of mouth.

3. How to find a partner

Before finding one, you should ask, do I need one? Carl Schramm suggests that having a partner increases the chances of failure as partners can get into a conflict which may turn fatal for the new venture. Schramm prefers to have good employees in the beginning. Schramm's approach presumes that the entrepreneur already has enough capital to afford an office, and salaries of employees, which is not always the case with startup entrepreneurs. You might lack sufficient capital so you might want to have a helping hand to distribute the workload or bring in some capital to invest as well.

Usually, it is your best friend or a friend who knows you well enough to trust you. Important thing is that all partners must believe in the same values, have the same vision, and the same degree of craziness. It will be extremely unlikely that you find a person randomly on social media, for example, and expect him to work with you with full commitment and zeal.

In the Memon community, for example, you will often find brothers, and cousins partnering together, taking capital from their parents to invest in a business. Do not take your sibling as a partner until he or she is as hardworking as you are.

Universities are a good place to find one. Educational institutions can be the best place to network with like-minded people. But you have to be social enough for that purpose. Challenge is that at a young age, with zero experience of working in the market, one may not be a very good judge of the character, and skill of people around. However, good universities do have societies that various events, and while becoming a part of their organizing team, one may acquire some skills to judge people. Also working under pressure in such a team enables you to not just evaluate your self but also other people as well.

Partners do not fall off from the sky, and it's better to have none, then to have a bad one ...

4. How to find a business idea

There can be at least three approaches to finding a business idea

- effectual way
- causal way
- through personal experience

The effectual way: This approach has already been explained earlier. It involves looking at your resources (skills, experience, contacts, capital, location, land, etc.), and working out what type of business one can build using the existing resources. This is the most pragmatic approach and can lead to results much quicker than other approaches.

The causal way

This approach attempts to find a market gap. This begins with analyzing market trends, and coming up with an emerging customer need or want which cannot be fulfilled with existing products or services in the market. This approach involves using scientific or statistical techniques to work out the details, and extent of the demand. The market size if found substantial, the product or services is which would fill the gap is considered viable. This approach involves too many theoretical assumptions and pushes the entrepreneur into hubris where it becomes difficult for him or her to realize the changing market dynamics or any mistake in the analysis. This approach often leads to inaccurate results but creates an impression of accuracy, and precision in analysis, often deluding the entrepreneurs, and investors about the hidden incorrectness. This approach must be avoided.

Through personal experience

This approach is perhaps more commonly used by entrepreneurs. When you experience a personal need (or problem), you often think or even develop a solution to address that need. The same solution may also be beneficial for others, so it is converted into a product or solution, and a business is built around the same to seamlessly deliver the solution to the others in need. The personal experience of going through pain or personal desire to solve the problem also becomes the driving force behind the entrepreneurial idea. The entrepreneur becomes passionate, and subsequently works harder, and with perseverance to convert his or her idea into a reality. The challenge is the lack of resources which the entrepreneur may not possess. So it may take a longer time to gather the resources necessary to convert the idea into a real business.

It is recommended that one may start a business first using the first option (effectual way), and once successful then divert the resources toward the idea emerging from the third option (through personal experience). One will not just have sufficient financial resources to experiment on the proposition, but will also have the necessary experience of building a business, which is a whole lot more crucial than financial capital. Another alternative to gain experience is to work for a small company operating in a market domain where your idea also fits in, finding such a job will not be easy of course. If you are lucky enough to have such a job then you can use the experience, and try to save some money, and then try to start your own company. But leaving a job after a few years of experience, when you may also have a family to feed is not going to be easy. The social pressures in Pakistan make it even more difficult.

Remember! A business idea is just to set your initial direction, it may change drastically as you move along. The problem you are trying to solve may remain there, but the product or service may change as per what the customer needs or what you can offer keeping in view your available resources. You must not become too emotionally attached to the product or service you may have worked hard to develop! Customer advice must be involved at every moment of product development. How this will be done, is explained next.

5. How to search for suppliers/vendors/ distributors in the international market?[9]

There are certainly many ways to expose your business to a pool of a vast number of suppliers and distributors. Below are some of the possibly most approachable or feasible ways to search for a suitable supplier for your need in general.

Trade Shows / Exhibitions

When unsure or starting from the very beginning, this seems more often as an option to expose one's business to the market representation of people attending shows or exhibitions, because these expose you to more suppliers, distributors, and even customers. All you have to do is to choose carefully the type of trade show or exhibition you want to display your business or product to because it should highly relate to it otherwise it's of no use to search for vendors that bring no significant value to your business. *Example:* If your business is about any FMCG brand, one may look for international exhibitions like Gulf-food-Exhibition that is hosted in Dubai each year connecting you to almost all suppliers from 40-60 countries related to ingredients, processing, packaging, and distribution.

Online Reliable Sources

A few trusted online trading platforms such as Amazon, Ali Baba or tdctrade.com, also help you build a network of suppliers, and manufacturers around your business as soon as you start a conversation

---

[9] Written by Muhammad Salman Farooq

with them. Other than that there are online trading directories available for easier search of your desired suppliers in respective domains.

Contacting local agents

Many international suppliers have their agents that one may contact before actually making a move to meet the owner or concerned designation of that party. These local agents can highly assist one to share with you their company's capabilities, specialties, and extra services that can add value to your business.

These were just some of the ways to approach or come in contact with a potential supplier; however, businesses need to locate a suitable supplier out of many. So the criteria or the selection process should follow the following possible steps that will ensure, and minimize the risks regarding appropriate vendor selection.

- Do they meet your anticipated standards of packaging, quality, price, and distribution?
- Research regarding their goodwill reputation in the market.
- Research their company from top to down i.e. from production to retailing.
- Communication barriers such as languages.
- Payment terms, and procedures that include credit terms, and liaison with concerned banks.
- Logistical procedures such as shipment process.
- Legal jurisdiction regarding insurance, defects, and who will be liable to pay for them at each stage of the process, demurrage charges (in case the ship loader fails to load or discharge the shipment in due time).

6. How to Import in Pakistan?[10]

Note: Readers from other countries may want to interview some local importers or clearing agents to understand the details of the import process

The import procedure starts with the purchase inquiry that which companies in the world are producing the required goods (getting a quotation from the supplier; RFQ (RequestForQuote). The importer may acquire all the main details from trade directories, and trade associations (http://www.dgto.gov.pk/). When obtaining the specified data, the importer communicates with the firm that is exporting goods to understand their rates and terms of delivery. Then the supplier issues "Proforma Invoice" against the request for a quote. A Pro forma invoice is a preliminary bill of sale sent to the importing company (buyers) in advance of a shipment or delivery of goods. The invoice will typically describe the purchased items details, rates, delivery time, shipping weight, and transport charges, etc.

Order Placement: After discussing all the valid points, and agreeing on terms, and conditions from both sides of the parties the sale/purchase legal contract is formed. Importer prepares the Purchase Order. The importer must obtain the foreign exchange rates (from the national bank or from the bank through which payments will be done afterward) for the payment purpose. The importer places the order for the product from the exporter of the foreign country. The order details contain quality, price, color, quantity, etc. of the product all the terms, and conditions (like mode of

---

[10] Written by Shamsher Ali

delivery, shipment By Sea or By Air / Payment terms / Expected Delivery date / Origin / Port of Discharge), etc.

Logistics is to decide the terms of shipment with your buyer. Usually, FOB (Freight on Board) is the common method in which the seller will deliver the goods up to the port of departure in the exporting country, and hand them over to the buyer's shipping agent. Then from there, the importer will have to bear all the freight and shipment costs of the goods. Another possible arrangement could be EXW (Ex-works/Ex-factory) in which the customer would pick up the goods from the supplier's factory, and all the costs of delivery up to his country will be borne by the buyer; and CIF (Cost, Insurance, Freight) in which all the cost, insurance, and freight of the goods will have to be borne by the exporter until the goods are received by the importer in his warehouse. In Karachi, the export through sea route is from Port Qasim, Kemari, and West Wharf, and for air route export is done through Jinnah International Airport.

Letter of Credit: After the order placement, and agreement of the payment term between the buyer, and seller, then the importer should acquire the letter of credit from his bank. This letter shows the credibility of the payment. For opening a letter of credit, the documents required include an agreement between Importer & Exporter, Proforma invoice, purchase order, details of exporter's bank, and insurance policy with a premium payment receipt. The importer has to keep a certain amount of money in his account for payment to the exporter's bank. Once the Letter of credit is opened it will be transmitted to the exporter's bank through SWIFT (Society for International Financial Telecommunication) which then forwards it to the exporter so that he manufactures the goods. Once the goods are shipped, the exporter provides the documents to the exporter's bank which includes a bill of lading, commercial invoice, packing list, certificate of origin, etc. The exporter's bank forwards these documents to the importer's bank. Once the importer's bank gets the documents it will make the payment from the importer's account through SWIFT to the exporter's bank. After making payment, Importer's bank provides those documents to the importer so that he can take the delivery of the goods from the port.

Following are the other methods of payments available for importers

Cash in advance/prepayment: Wire transfers and credit cards are the most commonly used cash-in-advance options available

Documentary collections/drafts/bills of exchange: A documentary collection (D/C) is a transaction whereby the exporter entrusts the collection of payment to the exporter's bank (remitting bank), which sends documents to the importer's bank (collecting bank), along with instructions for payment.

Open account: An open account transaction is a sale where the goods are shipped, and delivered before payment is due, which is usually in 30 to 90 days. This option is the most advantageous option to the importer in terms of cash flow, and cost, but it is consequently the highest risk option for an exporter

Consignment: Under the consignment method, a retail merchandiser acts as a consignor for goods supplied by the consignee. The consignor doesn't pay in advance for the consignee's goods. Instead, the consignor pays the consignee after the sales of goods and keeps a percentage of the proceeds.

Arranging payment: The importer needs to arrange all the payment before the arrival of the product at the port.

Note No advance for any product except health instruments, and health medicine, and it is limited to a maximum of 10,000 $ only.

The advice of Shipment, and other documents: It is the letter from the exporter to the importer informing about the complete details of the shipment like a packing list, vessel number (in case shipment by ship) or airway bill number (in case of air freight), the port of export, description of the product, bill of lading, and invoice number, insurance, and warranty certificates, certificate of origin to his banker for their forward transactions to the importer when he receives the bill of exchange drawn by the provider.

After product shipment, the exporter compiles the important documents, and provides it to the banker for further transfer, as mentioned in the letter of credit. Coordinate with the bank to get imports registered under Bank Contract / Collection, and generate the EIF (Electronic Import Form) required for both bank, and Pakistan Customs in Weboc portal.

Goods Arrival at Port: After the shipment of the loaded goods arrives at the port, an ANF (Arrival Notification) is sent to the consignee (nominated in the bill of lading). The ship in charge informs and provides the documents regarding goods, and import general manifest to the dock officer. Once the consignee receives the ANF, they can then start the customs clearance process to file a Bill of entry. Once this Bill of entry is filed and stamped by customs, the consignee can approach the shipping line for the release of the cargo upon arrival of the ship.

Customs Clearance: The Endorsed Original Shipping documents are forwarded to the Clearing agent to get the clearing process started, file the bill of entry, and get the goods clear from Customs inspection.

Import General Manifest (IGM) number to the shipment is generated which helps to locate the shipment in customs. After issuing this number, the shipment is offloaded.

Note: Customs duties are paid to the customs office to get the goods released. Then Logistics is arranged to transport the goods to the warehouse. If the goods are not cleared within 14 days then detention and demurrage charges are applied by port authorities depending on the size of the container.

The consignee passes on this release document to his nominated haulage (the commercial process transportation of goods) contractor for the container to be delivered at their nominated destination for unpacking. In the case of carrier haulage, the shipping line automatically does the movement once the above docs have been received.

Once the container has been delivered to the nominated destination, and the cargo unpacked, the consignee has to return the empty containers to the depot nominated by the shipping line within the specified free days allowed. The shipping lines monitor the incoming stock into their depots daily and charge demurrage (fine on late return of container as per the individual lines tariff) to the consignees that deliver the empty containers to the depot later than the free days.

Goods arrival at Site: On Shipment receipt in Warehouse, the attendant checks, and verify, and Quantity, and Type of items present in the packing list.

After successful verification, the GR of the said consignment entered in System, and Landed Cost for the same then executed to record the items received.

Documents used in an import transaction:

Packing list: A packing list is a document that includes details about the contents of a package. The packing list is intended to let transport agencies, government authorities, and customers know the contents of the package. These details help each of these parties handle the package accordingly.

B/L – Bill of Lading: A document issued by a carrier, or its agent, to the shipper as a contract of carriage of goods. It is also a receipt for cargo accepted for transportation and must be presented for taking delivery at the destination. Among other items of information, a bill of lading contains

1. Consignor's, and consignee's name,
2. Names of the ports of departure, and destination,
3. Name of the vessel,
4. Dates of departure, and arrival,
5. Itemized list of goods being transported with packages, and kind of packaging,
6. Marks, and numbers on the packages,
7. Weight, and/or volume of the cargo,
8. Freight rate, and amount.

Invoice of shipment: When products are shipped internationally, the shipper will have to provide the buyer with a Commercial Invoice document. The buyer (importer) will use this invoice, and other shipping documents to get the products cleared through customs in the country of import.

To import goods, the following prerequisites are required:

- National tax number (NTN) registration from the federal board of revenue (FBR)
- Copy of CNIC/ Passport of Individual
- One Page of Business Letter Head Pad (crossed as X),
- Bank Account Certificate issued by the bank for the account maintained in the name of the business
- Incorporation certificate by Securities, and Exchange Commission of Pakistan (SECP) in case of a company
- Visit the Regional Tax Office along with documents
- Sales tax number(STN) registration from the regional tax office
- The bank account of the applicant
- **Chamber of commerce registration from the district or city office:**
- A written application on business **letterhead** addressed to the Secretary-General LCCI/KCCI/ICCI/SCCI etc for grant of membership
- Filled in Membership Form, and Signature / ID Card Form
- Photocopy of C.N.I.C of the Proprietor
- Photocopy of Sales Tax Registration Certificate
- Photocopy of National Tax Number Certificate of the Proprietor
- Original bank certificate in the name of business applied for membership.
- Copy of a previous utility bill (gas/electricity/phone) paid from the business premises.

WEBOC registration (web-based one customs): It is a web-based system for filling Goods Declaration for Import cargo. Therefore for all the Importers WEBOC registration is MANDATORY.

- Sales Tax Number Copy
- National Tax Number Copy
- NTN Verification Copy
- CNIC Card Copy
- CNIC Nadra Verification
- ATL (Active Tax Payer) Copy
- Office Registry or Rent Deed Copy
- Bank Statement for the last three months. Original
- Bank account maintenance letter. Original
- One Utility Bill of Office
- **Letterhead** x 3 Copies

All the above documents are submitted to Deputy/Assistant Collector WEBOC USER ID SECTION

- Personal appearance of the applicant before the Deputy / Assistant Collector User-ID Section with original CNIC.
- Process of taking a digital picture, and thumb impression of the applicant upon personal appearance.
- The appraisers also visit the office premises for inspection, and after that, they approve for WEBOC.

Bank Account: Current Account is needed for import procedure and documentation.

Getting Import License: Not all goods require the import license; just a few of them are subject to the import license. So, the importer must get all the knowledge about the import-export policy to know about the policy of the goods whether it requires an import license or not.

7. How to export from Pakistan?[11]

Note: Readers from other countries may want to interview some local exporters to understand the details of the export process

Finding Customers

For a new entrant, who has not exported ever in his life, the biggest challenge is finding relevant customers and companies for his/her products. There are usually four traditional ways of finding customers, and marketing in export markets;

- The first is trade shows/exhibitions. Usually, trade shows are arranged all over the world. You rent a stall, showcase your product there, and get the maximum possible orders by giving discounts or other promotion tactics. The second benefit of having a stall in an international trade show is that you meet potential new customers, and can convert those potential customers into actual customers by a consistent sales, and marketing effort e.g. keeping in touch with them through emails, WhatsApp, sending promotional items, offering discounts, and if possible, meeting them personally at least once a year.

- The second way is to find a list of possible potential customers through trade organization websites. Every trade category in the world has its country-specific or global trade organization. You can Google the trade organization of your relevant category by using relevant keywords e.g. trade organization, association, etc, and check their website's members section to find your potential customer companies.

---

[11] Written by Nabeel Azeem

- The third way, which is a bit more traditional is to go to your local chamber of commerce, and ask them to give the specific trade directory of that category or country in which you are interested, get the list of your industry-specific relevant companies, and then contact them with your specific product offering. The fourth way is to have a sales team, either commission-based or full time, in your target country. You can find salespeople through local job sites.

- The fifth and most modern way is to market through online B2B trade portals e.g. Alibaba.com. Alibaba.com is the world's biggest online wholesale trade portal for small companies, and traders. Ali Baba group is valued at around 200 billion dollars. If you register there and pay a small fee they also give you a verified, and gold supplier status by physically verifying your company documents and office which adds credibility to your company name. You may not be able to get big orders from there, but you may be able to get small orders, and small fish captured together can make a big fish.

- Another possible option is to market directly to international big chains in your target country/region e.g. Walmart, Tesco, or Metro, etc. You can also sell to Amazon directly as it gives the option of bulk buying without selling your goods directly to consumers. For that, you need to have a partner outside Pakistan who has a registered company in your target market. Similarly, selling at E–bay also requires having a partner outside Pakistan in one of those countries where it is currently operating.

Feasibility

Feasibility is a detailed document which outlines all the important elements needed to start a business e.g. the cost of your product, the current price in the export markets, and the gross margins, the growth rate of the sector, important competitor countries, and major export markets, a possible production method for your product, financial projections, etc. For export, knowing your global competitor's rates is very important to compete with them. You can easily do that by finding the contact information of your competitor companies from trade directories or the internet and asking them the rates as a customer.

An important mistake which people make is they think that they can only start an export business by manufacturing. It is not true. You can also start exporting your product as a marketing company or a third-party manufacturer. In this arrangement, you have the export order, you buy the product from the manufacturer, and export it to your customer. The benefit of this arrangement is that in the beginning when you have few orders you do not have to pay the huge overhead of a manufacturing unit. Once when you start getting sufficient orders to sustain the overhead payments, then you can start your manufacturing.

The second way in the modern world is retail export. Retail export has been made possible in the world thanks to the global connectivity provided by the internet. In the retail export, you do not sell out the products at the wholesale price, instead, you sell them at the retail rate with a huge profit margin. In this case, even if your number of customers is small, still then you can reap healthy profits because of the huge margin per unit.

HS code, and the Taxes

HS code is the key thing that you will need to know for your export. HS code means a harmonized system of international classification which classifies every traded item with a number like 2018.4044 and based on this number, the duties, and taxes are assigned to every imported product. The first four numbers represent the specific category of that product e.g. plastics, metal, etc, and the second number represents the specific subcategory for that product. Your customer will ask you about your product's HS code so you should know about it.

Secondly, you should know the duties, value-added tax, or any other sales tax which will be levied on your product. If there is any export rebate offering, PTA (Preferential Trade Agreement), or FTA (Free Trade Agreement) of Pakistan with that country, you should know about it to maximize the value both for yourself, and your customer as well.

Logistics

Logistics are the backbone of international trade. You should know how your item will be shipped to your destination country; by sea or by air. Usually, high volume items with low prices per unit are exported through the sea, and high value but low weight items are exported through the air. The cost of your shipment is measured in terms of CBM. CBM stands for a cubic meter which is the standard size for which you will be charged for your shipment. You can divide your number of cartons or number of units per product which makes one cubic meter to calculate the shipping cost per unit. Along with that, you will have to pay your customs clearing agent, pay the relevant duty, hand over the relevant documents to your customer's shipping agent, and you are done. The documents which are needed are the invoice, packing list, and the bill of lading.

The next step in logistics is to decide the terms of shipment with your buyer. Usually, FOB (Freight on Board) is the common method in which the seller will deliver the goods up to the port of departure in the exporting country, and hand them over to the buyer's shipping agent. Then from there, the importer will have to bear all the freight and shipment costs of the goods. Another possible arrangement could be EXW (Ex-works/Ex-factory) in which your customer would pick up the goods from your factory, and all the costs of delivery up to his country will be borne by him; and CIF (Cost, Insurance, Freight) in which all the cost, insurance, and freight of the goods will have to be borne by the exporter until the warehouse of the importer.

In Karachi, the export through sea route is from Port Qasim, Kemari, and West Wharf, and for air route export is done through Jinnah International Airport.

Payment Methods

Once you get the order from your prospective buyer then the next thing is to decide on the payment terms. The most preferred payment term is LC (Letter of Credit) in which the buyer's bank gives you the payment guarantee in case if the buyer defaults or refuses to give you the payment on any grounds. The other possible options are D/C (Documents against Payment), and D/A (Documents against Acceptance). In D/C, the documents for releasing the shipment are received by your customer's bank, and they will only give them to your buyer if he/she has paid the cash for shipment to the bank. In documents against acceptance, the importer agrees to pay after a certain period e.g. 90 days once the required documents for shipment release have been released. The last possible option is an open account method in which the goods are shipped, and delivered before payment is due, which is usually in 30 to 90 days. Usually, D/P, D/A, and the open account are the riskiest options for a new exporter as there is no payment guarantee in these payment terms. However, some financial institutions also give credit insurance to your shipment, and export finance facility as well. If you have the export order, they will give you the money to finance your current financial needs for export order preparation, and then they will receive the payment from the customer on your behalf. DS Concept is one of the international companies providing export finance facilities in Pakistan.

Documents Required

The following documents are required for the processing of export.

- E-Form (from the authorized commercial bank)
- Commercial invoice
- Certificate country of origin
- Packing list
- B/L or AWB
- Non-GMO certificate (selected countries)
- Pre-shipment certificate (if needed)

COMMERCIAL INVOICE

SELLER		INVOICE NUMBER	DATE
		CUSTOMER REFERENCE NUMBER	DATE
SOLD TO		TERMS OF SALE/	
		TERMS OF PAYMENT	
SHIP TO		CURRENCY OF SETTLEMENT	
		MODE OF SHIPMENT	BILL OF LADING/AWB

QTY	PRODUCT DESCRIPTION AND HARMONIZED CODE	UNIT OF MEASURE	UNIT PRICE	TOTAL PRICE

PACKAGE MARKS	TOTAL COMMERCIAL VALUE	
	MISC CHARGES (PACKING, INSURANCCE, ETC.)	
	TOTAL INVOICE VALUE	

CERTIFICATIONS	I CERTIFY THA THTE STATED EXPORT PROCES AND DESCRIPTION OF GOODS ARE TRUE AND CORRECT
	SIGNED
	TITLE _____

Packing List

SHIPPER NAME AND ADDRESS			MARKS		
CONSIGNEE NAME AND ADDRESS					
			BOL / AIR WAYBILL NUMBER		
INVOICE NUMBER		INVOICE DATE	ORDER NUMBER		EXPORTING CARRIER

GROSS WEIGHT (kg)	NET WEIGHT (kg)	DIMENSIONS H x W x L	QUANTITY	DESCRIPTION

BILL OF LADING – NON-NEGOTIABLE

SHIPPER		B of L NO.	
NAME			
ADDRESS			
CITY / STATE / ZIP			
SID NO.			
SHIP TO		CARRIER NAME	
NAME		TRAILER NO.	
ADDRESS		SERIAL NOS.	
CITY / STATE / ZIP			
CID NO.			
THIRD PARTY FREIGHT CHARGES BILL TO		SCAC	
NAME		PRO NO.	
ADDRESS			
CITY / STATE / ZIP			
TELEPHONE			

SPECIAL INSTRUCTIONS

FREIGHT CHARGE TERMS
Freight charges prepaid unless marked otherwise.

PREPAID	COLLECT	THIRD PARTY

Master bill of lading with attached underlying bills of lading.

CUSTOMER ORDER NO.	NO. OF PKGS	WGT	PALLET / SLIP		ADDITIONAL SHIPPER INFO
			Y	N	
			Y	N	
			Y	N	
			Y	N	
TOTAL					

HANDLING UNIT		PACKAGE					LTL ONLY	
QTY	TYPE	QTY	TYPE	WGT	HM (X)	DESCRIPTION OF ARTICLES, SPECIAL MARKS & EXCEPTIONS	NMFC NO.	CLASS

Where the rate is dependent on value, shippers are required to state specifically in writing the agreed or declared value of the property as follows: "The agreed or declared value of the property is specifically stated by the shipper to be not exceeding _____ per _____.

COD AMOUNT $		
FEE TERMS		
COLLECT	PREPAID	CUSTOMER CHECK

NOTE: Liability limitation for loss or damage in this shipment may be applicable. See 49 USC § 14706(c)(1)(A) and (B).

Received, subject to individually determined rates or contracts that have been agreed upon in writing between the carrier and shipper, if applicable, otherwise to the rates, classifications, and rules that have been established by the carrier and are available to the shipper, on request, and to all applicable state and federal regulations.

The carrier shall not make delivery of this shipment without payment of charges and all other lawful fees.

SHIPPER SIGNATURE

SHIPPER SIGNATURE & DATE	CARRIER SIGNATURE & PICK-UP DATE	TRAILER LOADED	
		BY SHIPPER	
		BY DRIVER	
This is to certify that the above-named materials are properly classified, packaged, marked, and labeled, and are in proper condition for transportation according to the applicable regulations of the DOT.	Carrier acknowledges receipt of packages and required placards. Carrier certifies emergency response information was made available and/or carrier has the DOT emergency response guidebook or equivalent documentation in the vehicle. Property described above is received in good order, except as noted.	**FREIGHT COUNTED**	
		BY SHIPPER	
		BY DRIVER/PALLETS SAID TO CONTAIN	
		BY DRIVER PIECES	

107

Certificate of Origin

Exporter Name and Address	Blanket Period: (DD/MM/YYYY)
	FROM:
Tax Identification Number	TO:
Producer Name and Address	Importer Name and Address:
Tax Identification Number:	Tax Identification Number:

Description of Good(s)	TARRIF CLASSIFICATION NUMBER	PREFERENCE CREITERION	PRODUCER	NET COST	COUNTRY OF ORIGIN

I CERTIFY THAT:

- Information provided in this certificate is based on facts and is accurate and I assume the responsibility for proving such representations. I understand that I am liable for any false statement or material omission made on or in concern with this document.
- I agree to maintain and present upon request documentation necessary to support this certificate and to inform, in writing, al persons to whom this certificate was given of any changes that would affect accuracy or validity of this certificate.
- This certificate consists of _____ pages including all attachments

Authorized Signature:		COMPANY:	
Name: (Print or Type)		**TITLE:**	
Date: DD/MM/YYYY	**Ph:** xxxxxxxxxxxxxxx	**Fax:** xxxxxxxxxxxxxxxxxx	**Customs Form:**

8. How to build a prototype

Building a prototype depends on the nature of the product. Building a prototype of an automobile will be a different ball game, in comparison to building a prototype of a new design of a dress shirt. So the more technical a product, the more difficult it can become.

- For clothes, you may first want to sketch the designs on a piece of paper, and then take it to a tailor.
- For food items, it's a no brainer, you can use the kitchen, and use the help of a more experienced cook which can even be your mom.
- For software packages, for example, one may design the layout in PowerPoint (using hyperlink function), or Photoshop or any other image editing software to demonstrate to the customer.
- For a physical product that may involve metal or plastic parts, one first has to develop a fully functional 3D model in an engineering visualization software like Solidworks, ProEngineers, SolidEdge, or Catia, etc. Before making a 3D model, try sketching it on a piece of paper then go for 3D. Once done, a 3D printer or an actual fabrication technique can be used to build a prototype.
- For metal fabrications, it's better to use a pipe structure, and sheet metal because of the relative ease of construction.

Avoid making complicated metallic parts which may involve CNC machines. If unavoidable, you can use wood instead of metal, and use a CNC milling machine to cut the wooden log into your desired shape. But for that, you must make sure that your 3D model contains all the nth level details, no matter how insignificant they appear.

But before spending a lot of money on the prototype, you must first ask 100 times, why you want to build it yourself? It often requires millions of rupees just to develop a new product like that! Do you have a facility to mass-produce the product? Is there enough demand in the market to justify the investment? Is there an existing product in the local or international market which serves a similar purpose? Usually, companies with a running business, with lots of cash in hand, try to adventure into new areas like this! In other countries, inventors often spend years to build a prototype and then outsource their production to an existing manufacturer. In Pakistan, the manufacturing base is not strong enough, while in China what is the guarantee that your idea will not get stolen? So there are a lot of ifs, and buts, and questions, so make sure you have done your homework properly before investing a fortune into a venture which makes you walk through this minefield.

9. How to validate a business idea

A product or service idea is validated using customer feedback. The problem is customer or user feedback if taken without showing the actual product, or without letting them experience the product first hand, can be misleading.

So instead of just talking to the customers or users about hypothetical features of your proposition, involve some of them right from the time when you are developing a product. Or if you are providing a service, find a customer or a few, who can let you deliver the service to them. Deliver the service to them for free as a sample, if possible. Once you engage the customer in real-time, he or she can provide more realistic feedback on how to fine-tune the product. The customer must be willing to use the product or service to give you feedback in case it serves their needs.

You may put yourself in the shoes of the customer, or involve your family members or friends depending on if the product or service is of some use to them. Engaging the customer or the user in the product development process is the key.

Once the product or service is fine-tuned, try now selling it to some actual customers, again by using your network. The goal again is to find out how a new customer would react to it. Do not begin to mass-market the product or service at this time. If you can sell the product to a few customers, provide them the best customer service possible. So that they may feel comfortable in case if a problem or point of dissatisfaction arises while using the product or service. Take their feedback, and further refine or evolve the product as suggested, if deemed necessary.

Through this iterative process, you will be able to reach a point where the product or service, along with its packaging, and the delivery mechanism will be ready to be mass-marketed.

But before that, you need to work out if you will be able to deliver the product or service in larger quantities, which means you must develop a system (how to) to deliver the right product in the right quantity at the right price to the right customer.

How to fail cheaply, and quickly

The idea is to spend less money, resources, and time to find out if the proposition you have developed will be acceptable to your target audience. First, you need to work out your affordable loss. This is the amount of money, time, and other resources that you are comfortably willing to lose to test your proposition. It should be around 10-20% of your total savings in terms of money, but it would vary from person to person.

Once you have worked out your affordable loss, see what is the minimum viable product or service design you can develop. A minimum viable design is the one that is capable of satisfying the customer needs you are targeting at a very basic level. You can minus the packaging or any aesthetic features if they are not directly meant to serve the customer's needs.

The goal here is to test the concept, and not to sell the product to the customer.

10. How to identify the target audience

Ideally, you should have already met your customer before starting the business. The idea behind your product or service should emerge from your one-on-one interaction with the customer. You can be a potential customer of the product (assuming if someone else is selling it) if you have conceived it in the light of a personal need or challenge.

Now you need to generically define who is your customer, for example, you might say they are housewives, in their mid-30s or 40s, have at least 3 kids, who live in Gulistan-e-johar, and who also know how to drive, or do not want to cook food, etc.

You need to be as specific as possible, as you will talk to one target segment at a time when you will attempt to advertise your product. Your selling pitch will use a language that suits a specific group. A product that is designed for software engineers will be pitched differently as compared to a product designed for farmers.

Do not hypothetically assume that a specific segment in the market would want to buy your product or service. It is also entirely possible that once you begin to market your product, you may discover an entirely new type of market segment who may want to use your product more than the segment you initially attempted to target. One has to be focused, and open-minded at the same time; focusing on the needs of a single segment, while opening the door for the new ones to arrive.

It is entirely possible that the kind of people whose input you involved in the product development process, might not be as interested as a new customer segment. If so, then your work on product development has not been finished as yet, in fact, it never will. As with the emergence of every new kind of target segment, you may have to modify your proposition as per the demands of potential customers. It is an ongoing iterative process, and the ones who are adaptable, have a good listening ability, and the capacity to empathize with the customers are the ones who can keep evolving as required.

Use of Intuition, gut feel is fundamentally important in knowing if you are headed toward the right kind of customers.

11. How to avoid/resolve a conflict between partners

Conflicts are primarily a result of misunderstandings, and misunderstand results with miscommunication, while miscommunication happens when agreements are often done verbally in unclear terms, or with disregard to the possibility of misinterpretations. This seldom happens because of ill-intentions, and if ill-intention is the cause then it would not be possible to avoid even if all communication, particularly related to the conditionality of an agreement between partners is done in writing, let alone on stamp paper, or even in the presence of witnesses, and a layer.

So the character and honesty of intention is a prerequisite in any business relationship. Ability to execute as per commitments is another necessary trait as mere being nice does not suffice; an incapable partner will eventually fall short of his or her commitment and would keep excusing., and persistent lack of commitments can eventually lead to a potential conflict.

So finding the right partners becomes critically important, and there is no formula to guarantee if the person will fall short of his or her expectations. We cannot even say this for our selves. What is important is a mixture of character, honesty, capability, persistence, and commitment which if present would eventually lead to smooth business relations.

The tendency to over-commitment is another possible cause of conflict, as this would lead to miss commitments, and thus toward conflict. Over-commitments could be a result of lack of self-awareness, and personal insecurities, as often people who overcommit are unable to set boundaries and find it difficult to say no when they have to.

So the key is to avoid people who are insecure, ill-intended, dishonest, and it is recommended that they are tested before taking on board as a partner. This testing is often done with smaller assignments or deals, and if they can fulfill their smaller commitments, then gradually they may be tested with bigger commitments. Often suppliers in the market test the new buyers likewise, and after a few deals they decide if they can offer supplies on credit, and if the buyer keeps honoring his or her commitments then the supplier keeps increasing the credit amount to the extent possible for them. It has been noted that often the relationship reaches a level where there is blind trust between suppliers, and their buyers (in a B2B context), and suppliers even supply more than what is asked even on credit because of the confidence they have in their buyers.

So now if the conflict has arrived, then the first cardinal rule to easily resolve is to look for misunderstanding or miscommunication, instead of doubting or judging the intentions of the other partner. As more than often the cause of a conflict is not in the ill-intentions rather in miscommunications or some other genuine unavoidable reasons. So if this principle is adopted, then eventually every conflict could be resolved by clearing the miscommunication which might have happened.

Miscommunication can also be due to a third person who might be feeding information to one of the partners regarding the other. So before entertaining such incoming pieces of information, it may be necessary to verify what this third person has said. Back bitters also need to be eliminated from the system when necessary.

Once the miscommunication has been resolved, then it may be necessary to ensure to eliminate the cause of miscommunication that may happen again in the future. Like writing down the terms of agreement paper, and agreeing on every aspect of the contract before proceeding with the actual business.

Excess profits and excess loss in business are often a source of conflict among partners when it has not been decided earlier regarding what to do in case if excess profits are to be reinvested or transferred to the personal accounts of partners, or in case of excess loss who will bear it, and in what proportion. Conflict due to excess profits and excess loss may happen in particular when partners' level of commitment is not equal like one is spending more time, while the other is not. To avoid this, quantification of responsibilities and level of involvement in business in measurable terms may be necessary, in advance.

In the end, it all depends on the character, and how big the hearts of both partners, and if they tend to doubt the intentions, then even self-fulfilling prophecy (when our expectations influence the behavior of the other person, and when the other person behave as we expected, we exclaim, aha!) can turn the partners against each other despite no genuine reason.

12. How to find angel investors?

An angel investor is an investor who invests without much strings attached. Mostly angel investors are found in friends, and family, and rarely among strangers who you can touch with your passion. Greg Mortenson for example wrote about finding such an angel investor for his school project by writing letters to hundreds of wealthy, and famous people, and one of them responded, and gave him the right amount. Greg Mortenson had a strong social cause and was able to demonstrate his commitment toward that cause. However, Mortenson's story is not common. GEM (Global Entrepreneurship Monitor) survey and other research on the subject reveal that around 50-60% of the money entrepreneurs around the world can find within friends and family.

However, before looking for investment, please read the first half of this book, and evaluate whether you need investment in the first place or not. If you are looking for investment without experience and starting something on a very small scale then please reevaluate what you are trying to do.

So in case if you have evaluated your options and plan, and you do need some financial injection, then see if anyone in your family or friends can do that. Ask yourself this question, what if I have the money, and someone comes to me asking for investment, why would I give it to him or her? What questions would I ask, what would I look for?

An obvious reply would be the dedication, and commitment of the person and evidence convinces the angel investor about your dedication, and commitment. Also, your record would matter. Most likely the investor would already know you personally or through a strong reference. So have your record sound enough to establish credibility.

All of this is being said keeping in view if there is such a person in your network who has enough to invest and is eager to invest as well. Often when people start a business, and it grows to an extent, people automatically come forward with proposals to invest, and partnership.

If this happens, and it may happen more than often, then the tables would turn for you, and you will rather be in a position where you will have to evaluate if it would be safer, and beneficial for you (keeping in view the psychological pressure an investment brings), and your business or not.

If the tables turn, ask then you must be very sure about the exit strategy! You must agree with the content of it in writing with the incoming investor. It is the strategy of ending a business relationship in case if the business fails or the investor wants to bail out for whatever reason even if the business is running alright. It would be better to involve, and discuss a corporate lawyer here, and do necessary legal paperwork even if the amount is not large enough.

Often businesses collapse just because an investor wants to bail out, and the entrepreneur has to sell a considerable amount of fixed assets or inventory without which the business cannot operate. So to avoid any such scenario, prior terms in writing need to be agreed, like to draw back the investment the investor would take small installments which would be a percentage share in profit, etc.

Please recall the importance of trust in every business relationship, which I explained above (see 'How to build credibility?' on page 75). Without truth, this particular relationship between an investor, and entrepreneur cannot also work, particularly when the investor has trust issues. Also as an entrepreneur, you must always try to avoid any activity which may create doubts in the heart of the investor. Investors are also like partners, and to avoid any conflict with them please see the chapter on avoiding, and resolving conflicts (see page 115).

13. How to price the product?

Before working out the selling price, do you exactly know how much your product costs you? This should include costs like that of raw material, transportation, any other utility expenses, rent of your office, the salary of your employees, your income, any other overhead costs, etc. Often it takes a while to truly determine exactly how much it costs you.

It is better to avoid incurring any fixed costs, or investment in the assets unless you are confident that you will be able to recover the investment. This confidence must only be based on your experience of selling to the customer. If you have a strong growing customer base, now you may think of investing in some real assets. Not before. Ask yourself do I have a number based on my experience on which I will amortize my fixed cost?

Once you have calculated your cost, while not ignoring the govt. taxes, now you know at what selling price you will be able to incur a loss or profit.

- Look at the competitors or substitute products, to see where you should place your price.
- Look at how desperately the customer wants a product (not in the sense to exploit a customer's pain point)
- Look at the value of the problem you attempt to solve through your product or service, without becoming greedy
- Look at the general buying power of your customer base
- You must also consider that you must not make the customer feel ripped off after buying your product or service
- Use your gut feel.

You might have to experiment with different price points with different customers to come to an optimum selling price. This must be done before the mass marketing of the product.

If you arrive at a price that is less than your cost, then either you have to cut down your cost or have to find a customer base that can pay for it, or let go of the product or service altogether.

If it's a similar product to what is already available then working out a cost is not much of a hassle.

The right approach should be to see what the customer can pay and then tweak your proposition to develop an offering.

Product packaging and presentation also plays a very important role in charging a premium from the customer. But the product quality and customer experience must also be worthy of its packing to ensure repeat sales.

14. Start-up hiring strategy[12]

Whenever a new business starts the entrepreneur is the only person who is working on all aspects of the business or maybe the founding members if the business is started by more than one individual. Once the business is in place, hiring employees to perform certain tasks is done to ensure smooth business operation, and every business, whatever its nature may be, requires employees to keep performing in the growth phase otherwise there is a significant chance that the business growth may stagnate, and eventually decline without the venture ever reaching its potential.

Things may vary depending on the nature of the business but generally, a business that operates on the storefront or brick, and mortar model will require a market presence with a physical shop location, and store requires sales staff, cashiers, etc. generally a basic store has a single owner who operates the whole business expansion leads to the hiring of an employee to look after the store in the absence of the owner, and the model may change in case of larger stores with multiple salespeople, and cash handling, and billing people.

Businesses that operate on the online model may not require employees upfront, and they may be able to operate for a longer period under sole operation by the owner since the physical presence at a location is not required.

---

[12] Written by Razi Uddin, and Faizan Abdul Khaliq

Hiring the first employee

When hiring an employee, the entrepreneur must

- Know the budget available, and number of job positions required
- Assess whether they need a single person to perform multiple job roles or whether to hire multiple people for specialized roles

Generally, when the first employee is hired the business has not taken off, and budget constraints are present it is advisable to hire an employee who may be paid well but can perform expertly in multiple roles. For example, instead of managing only material purchasing the person should be able to oversee the end to end operations including HR or instead of just acting as head of sales he must be able to perform as head of marketing, and business development as well.

In the case of shop fronts, the person must be capable enough to perform multiple tasks required in the store. In the case of online businesses, the employee must be able to perform all technology-related tasks in addition to the basic operations of the business.

Qualities to seek in an employee

The first rule of startup hiring is to never hire an employee with no experience in your line of work or in the task you want to be performed by them. You are hiring an employee to make your work easier, this means you already have little time to spare so you won't be able to train them extensively, and would want them to start delivering almost instantly. In case of a fresh hire this would not be the case they would require to be trained, and while they are learning the tasks the workload of the entrepreneur increases as he has to perform all the tasks in addition to training the employee. A fresh employee can also underperform therefore may incur a hidden cost to the business.

It is important to do cost-benefit hiring, hire someone who can perform multiple roles, and be able to multitask. This will provide an edge as a startup cannot afford to hire multiple persons, and getting the most out of a single person will benefit the business greatly. Sometimes paying a person slightly higher pay will get you the tasks done for two people at the price of 1.25 persons.

Whenever hiring a full-time employee ensure that this job is their bread and butter, and they are not working elsewhere after hours or have a supplementary job or venture. This may sound obnoxious but working at a startup is hectic, and employees may be required to put in extra hours, work late, come early, and any person who is not invested fully in the venture will find it hard to give time to all parallel ventures, and your business will suffer due to their underperformance.

Part-time employees

When hiring part-time workers which would certainly be the case when the business is in its early stages, and full-time employees cannot be afforded the part-time employee must have a pre-decided work schedule where they are available to you for a pre-decided number of full days. Half days might work for some roles while not for others. You can afford a part-time accountant but a part-time salesperson is not usually feasible. Business support related tasks like HR, purchasing, accounting can be managed initially by the part-time staffers. The roles and responsibilities must be predefined, and the amount of time, and performance management indicators must also be decided for part-time employees at the start of their employment to ensure that business does not suffer due to their status as a part-time employee.

Part-time or full-time employee versus the task outsourced

It is also necessary to see if it is necessary to hire a person part-time for a job or could the job be outsourced for a lesser cost. For example, hiring an accountant may be expensive as compared to an accounting firm handling your accounting for example hiring an accountant may be expensive as compared to an accounting firm handling your accounting for you.

How to hire candidates

There are multiple options for hiring the required talent. Head hunters can be used, LinkedIn, social media networking, websites like OLX also provide platforms for job seekers, and employers to find each other free of cost, referrals from within social circles can also be used these are the most common ways for looking up talent as a startup. If you cannot find your required talent through these ways, poaching talent from the competition can be done. This will provide you with an experienced individual who is aware of the job role, and the sector as well. This requires identifying, and having a personal interaction with the intended talent that has to be poached, and persuade them to join you.

In the case of small businesses for example a cosmetics shop owner who requires a salesman can hire a salesman working for another shop in the same or different market by personally approaching them. These personal calls may provide you with the required person or get a referral of a person who is equally experienced, and willing to switch.

Whenever hiring, assess the employee on the skills, and credentials required as well as their suitability to your way of operating business, and your work culture. Market reputation is generally available for most people, and it is not difficult to know their professional standing in the market, and it is suggested to research the candidate before finalizing the hiring.

Retaining employees

Startups cannot afford high employee turnovers yet most startups have employees leaving rapidly. To retain employees, it is difficult being a startup to be able to offer the best compensation in the market but employees can be retained by motivation and engagement. Providing frequent motivation, and engagement as well as development opportunities to engage, and provide them with a sense of belonging with the organization will foster loyalty. Their pay can be designed to offer target based bonuses or commissions to motivate them to perform and meet the targets required.

Salaries can also be designed to account for certain allowances that will motivate the employee to perform the required tasks. For example, giving a fuel allowance to a sales employee will be a good investment since now you can require him to travel over long distances within his assigned area without him complaining of fuel expenses.

Turning employees into assets

It is important to have your employees invested in the success of the venture. Employees who won't be impacted by the loss in business will never be a true asset since they will not have a stake in the good or bad of the company. Employees who share the same level of ownership to the business as the owner will result in them investing all efforts for the betterment of the venture.

At the end of the day, the owner of the business cannot run the operation successfully without the support of the employees. The employees with the right credential who are the proper fit within the unit will provide the impetus required for growth and business development.

15. How to develop customer support or relationship management system?[13]

The level of customer engagement varies from industry to industry but there is a common goal, engage the customer. Build a connection with the customer, create that personal touch in the relationship between the brand or business, and the customer. The end goal you see is to keep existing customers and create word of mouth to get new business through referrals, and good faith in the market. Customer retention is extremely important for any business, and this is why they try to engage with the customers to let no customer go unsatisfied however some businesses master it better than others.

If we talk about the most basic customer relationship management the smiling salesperson on a shop that treats you politely obliges each of your requests, and treats you with respect stands a big chance to create a repetitive relationship with the customer. We have seen many salespeople that are charming enough for you to tolerate them but their greed to make a sale can be detected, and the sincerity that they portray can be detected by the seasoned customers as a façade just for making a sale. This phenomenon needs to be avoided when engaging with customers. A majority of customers know when they are being given sincere advice, and the customer relationship managers in most cases the salesperson must be sincere when it comes to dealing with customers. A customer deceived once can give a good return once but a customer whose heart has been captured will give exponential returns of years to come, and all successful

---

[13] Written by Faizan Abdul Khaliq, and Razi Uddin

businesses have managed to make it big due to an army of loyal customers. This is what a customer relationship manager, the person interacting with the customer should understand, embrace, and practice. Customer relationship in essence is a thankless job where the majority of the working day is focused on the problem, and conflict resolution, empathizing and removing the pain for the customers, dowsing water on metaphorical fires. The only definition for a job well done in customer relations is to always leave a customer happy, and satisfied

Our businesses are transitioning from traditional setups towards more modern brands, and companies, and it is the need of the hour for them to focus on customer relationship management more than ever. Although physical change is hard yet achievable, a change in the mentality is harder to achieve. The existing culture requires a shakeup from existing norms towards a more customer-centric focus of our business. Our business owners need to understand price, and quality matter but the catalyst to creating a repeat customer is always great customer service. With good price point, and quality your customers may be loyal but they will be hostages, doing business with you due to a lack of options, and given a choice will never prefer your service over a customer-focused competitor, and in most cases, the price point tends to get ignored a little, and a pricier option could be chosen just due to better service.

Setting up a CRM system

On an extremely basic level, spreadsheet software can offer the best platform for creating a CRM database for small businesses that are in their initial stages. This information can be stored on the cloud, and accessed, and edited via smartphone as well to enable ease of data entry, and provide safety of data due to sync to cloud features.

If we talk about how we can set up a CRM system, there are several options one can opt for depending on the scale of the requirement by the organization. There are several options available in the market for ready-made systems available that can be scaled to meet the needs for organizations Oracle, SAP, Salesforce, IBM, and several others are readily available. Considering cost factors locally made CRM systems can also be developed through local software houses that offer cost-effective solutions or have it made in-house by hiring the development team as employees to create, and maintain the system. The goal of setting up a CRM system is to create a customer database, and log all interaction for that customer, and log all information gathered related to that customer to enhance the knowledge a business has related to its customer this helps to upsell, and effectively target customers, and also be mindful of a customer's preferences. The cycle of data building starts when a customer interacts with the customer relations for the first time. Take examples of credit or debit cards that require activation over the phone, and this builds the first log in customer relationship records, moving this relationship forward the bank monitors the cash inflows, and product usage, and then sales representatives target customers with other financial products. A debit cardholder can sell personal loans, and credit cards, etc. If we take an example of pizza delivery they keep your phone number as an identifier, and previous order delivery address saved. Customer service calls also yield important information logs of which are kept in the customer's file.

One aspect of CRM is the software-based or cloud-based system the second more important factor is the human who is actively engaging with the customer be it via voice or text, and through whichever platform hiring the right fit, and training them is vital for the success of any system. The quality of talent available in the market remains an issue with CRM related jobs often not the best paying ones and not the first choice for most of the top talent in the market. Therefore, when you can't find what you want the best option is to mold what you have into what you want with the right training there is no doubt that this can be achieved, and this highlights why when setting up a CRM system a robust training program must be designed alongside to effectively manage, and help the system drive results.

Whenever a CRM system is installed it has to be able to deliver the required data with appropriate filters, and data analysis should be a matter of clicks. Simplicity is the key for interfaces especially in cases where the system is locally made the freedom for design modifications is far more as compared to commercial CRM solutions. In these cases, it is important to have the system experts, and the people responsible for decision making based on that system-generated data need to be aligned. Misalignment usually results in inefficiencies, and the long run poor performance.

CRM today

Today customer relationship management is transitioning towards social media relationship management. We see most brands have an active presence on social media platforms since today's generation engages more on social media as compared to emails and phones. Twitter, Facebook, WhatsApp for business, Instagram, and other social media platforms present companies an opportunity to engage with customers over social media, and provide a personalized experience, and increase the reach into the customer's phone.

Many brands have created chatbots on their Facebook pages to provide basic information instantly. Human controlled social media channels are also growing, and companies are increasingly becoming active on these platforms to engage customers with their evolving preferences. There is a growing recognition by companies that social media is the place where the majority of customer interaction will take place.

There is one thing that businesses need to understand that when they are in growth phase they need to create a CRM system that enables them to accommodate the increasing customer traffic, and also to enable businesses to effectively utilize the increasing amount of customer data that is available, and also the need to secure that data from other external forces as well.

CRM, and Information security

When a CRM system is created and managed the safety, and security of this database are extremely important. The database and the personal information of customers must remain safe, and this data must not reach unscrupulous hands. If customer data is breached and leaked the customer trust will be damaged irreparably for the business. In this regard selection of CRM systems, and their security must also be ensured by the business.

CRM, and data analysis

Businesses in Pakistan especially small, and medium scale enterprise are yet to extract ultimate value from CRM however a few that have done so are reaping benefits of the rich data generated by the hundreds of customer interactions, and analyzing that alongside sales, and market data to formulate customer-focused strategies that provide the customer with enhanced product experience, and allow for better targeting, and segmentation of customers. Especially for products where personal selling is important such as financial products can be targeted to a better-suited audience to get a higher proportion of fruitful results.

Challenges for CRM

The first, and foremost challenge for customer relationship management is our antiquated mentality of doing business. Most businesses are still operated by conservative management that is resistant to the status quo and tend to find it hard to leave their well-established norms, and transition towards a more digital, customer-focused model of doing business. It is hard to convince people that relationship management is required in all business sectors even monopolies like utility service providers need a good customer relationship system today because monopolies will never last, and at the end of the day business can generate greater value from satisfied customers as compared to disgruntled ones. Another challenge is the cost of setting up and operating an effective CRM system. Most of the options in off the shelf software are too expensive, and locally produced software may have reliability issues initially like all newly built ERP solutions that demand frequent troubleshooting and debugging the appetite for which does not exist in most business leaders. The third challenge that is faced in our market is that our businesses fail to gain the trust of the customer at times they try, and compensate for the gaps in customer service however at large people responsible for customer relationship are unable to serve the customers, there are many examples of promising ventures that are just lagging due to a mediocre customer relationship management.

How can we bridge the gaps?

Change is inevitable, with the next generations of traditional business owners coming into the family business, and actively taking over decision making roles. The direction for many businesses will shift for some the process has already begun. Similarly, Pakistan origin software that can reliably serve customer's needs for a CRM system, and not cost huge license fees will motivate business owners to invest in CRM. Most importantly a shift towards decision making based on data, and analytics will encourage the adoption of CRM systems to provide customer data for effective decision making, and strategy formulation.

16. How to develop systems to put a business on autopilot?

Before asking about system automation, let alone system development, we need to ask what kind of work needs to be systemized or replaced with automation?

Foucault once said that 'absence of work is madness', however, if we listen to Victor Frankle than meaningless work as well can have its toll on the human psyche, in fact in Frankliean context one can also argue for a case of meaningful idleness. Frederick Herzberg would also agree about the meaningful work, where one's micro contribution in the macro picture has a substantive value, like that Janitor who said proudly to US President John F. Kennedy that "I am helping put a man on the moon", or that laborer who argued that he isn't putting bricks to make a wall, rather building a cathedral. This is how one can see the bigger picture which gives meaning to our work. Likewise, there can be meaningless work as well, where one cannot see how his or her contribution adds to the bigger picture, like doing something only because the boss wants it to be done for some reason the boss did not explain. Or running after some performance numbers which the system thinks are important, but you know it for a fact that they aren't.

So while arguing for a case of systemizing or even automating the work, one needs to ask, whether the work which is being systemized or automated is a meaningful activity or a meaningless activity. If it's a meaningless activity, does it need to be performed in the first place, and if yes, then would it be cost-effective to deploy a standard operating procedure for it, let alone using some software to automate it. Secondly, if the work is indeed meaningful, depending on the meaningfulness of the ultimate purpose of the business, and if the employees do find it intrinsically motivating, then does the work need to be re-engineered in a way that it is no more dependent on a particular employee or a group of employees rather is systemized, or automated? One must not proceed without answering this question.

The idea of systemization is grounded in another presumption that humans, in general, cannot be trusted or are inherently incapable of consistent performance, let alone hard work, while the nature of output requires consistent performance from human employees. Also, that to produce the products or services with consistent quality, and required quantity, the process needs to be standardized. It is true that human beings do not operate as consistently as robots, but is such a consistency even required? Can the output tolerate a human level variation? Why is an artesian culture not suitable for the design of the organization? Why is a mass-production unit needed which would continuously produce large quantities of identical products? Why cannot there be some variation in output?

These questions point toward the very objective of the business, the nature of the product or service, the value proposition committed to the customer, the nature of competition in the market, and most importantly the very theory of the firm employed while establishing a business firm. Therefore there cannot be a simple yes, and no answer to the questions raised above.

On one hand, a business may look like a family, where human variability in output is not just accepted but part of the value proposition, generally the products or services referred to 'handmade' have such variability, and the customers or users value it even, as each product is though identical, and unique at the same time. On the extreme of the spectrum, each product can be highly customized as well.

On the other end of the spectrum, a business may look like a machine, where each variation follows a six-sigma approach, which implies that each product is perfectly identical to the other. Take iPhones as an email, or any cell phone model. However the employees in such systems are like machine components, and only there because they are cheaper than robots, or perhaps robots are not advanced enough at the moment. It is little surprise that Foxconn factories in China, where iPhones are assembled, have suicide nets across the buildings inside their facility to prevent the workers from committing suicide[14].

So shifting away from being people-centric, to system-centric is not just an economic decision, but also a moral one, with consequences on the lives of the people working in the business. However, it is also important to facilitate the employees in their repetitive or monotonous tasks through automation for example in a way that increases the empowerment, and ownership of the employee rather than making the employee irrelevant from the process.

The book called 'E-Myth' by David Gerber perhaps offers the simplest way to develop a system driven business in this context, however, even in this book the significance of the employee as an integral component of the system is marginalized, and rather the employee is seen as a component of the system. Nevertheless, the guideline provided in the book 'E-Myth' is centered around the idea of documenting the steps of the routine

---

[14] See this for details: https://en.wikipedia.org/wiki/Foxconn_suicides

processes, creating checkpoints, installing fail-safe wherever necessary, and deploying measures for accountability.

Often employees are manipulated in this context with measurable KPI, however, quantification or gamification, in particular, turns their job into a number game, while destroying their intrinsic motivation, and ownership in the job. Alternatively, the Toyota Production System may be studied in this context. Jeffery K. Liker's book The Toyota Way outlines 14 techniques employed by Toyota to run their system of production, which can be customized, and adapted anywhere. Interestingly, the Toyota Production System does that in a way that it does not kill the motivation of the employees rather makes them the central part of the entire improvement process.

Since this is a complex subject, and books are available on it, therefore, only some key consideration points are highlighted here. Readers are encouraged to go through the books mentioned above to further enlighten themselves.

17. How to become an authorized distributor of an established brand?[15]

This article shares information about different Distribution License Types intended to help potential entrepreneurs make better decisions while deciding the brand, and license type they aim to obtain. Further, this article provides insights on what an entrepreneur should expect when they reach out to a brand, what do international brands look for in a distributor, and how do they shortlist a distributor for official talks amongst multiple distribution proposals. With this information, an entrepreneur should be able to build a strong proposal/case for a distribution license.

Starting with distribution types, once you have figured out which product category you want to work with, evaluate the market before deciding the brand that you want to work with as you need to be aware of the current distribution status of your desired brand (referred to herewith as "Brand X"). There could be one or more of these following types of distributors which can be working for Brand X:

- Nationwide Exclusive Distributor
- Region Specific Distributor
- Product Specific Distributor
- No distributor at all

---

[15] Written by Zaid Hanif

Nationwide Exclusive Distributor

Nationwide exclusive distribution often results from the prior performance as a product and a history of a good working relationship. Obtaining such a license directly is possible only with very strong goodwill, and market penetration of the distributor company, which puts the distributor in a position where the distributor can demand a nationwide distribution license to start a business with the brand.

For an entrepreneur to seek distribution of a brand that already has a Nationwide Exclusive Distributor would be a task beyond worth the efforts, and time. In this case, apart from establishing the fact that your business is capable enough to operate an international brand, you will also be required to prove your ability to perform better than the current distributor.

Having said that there are examples in Pakistan where new companies have secured brands from established distributors, but it requires a heavy investment that could be in the form of an initial purchase that is equivalent to annual sales of the last distributor and further contract of high annual sales targets. If you wish to opt for a brand that already has a nationwide distributor, you need to have answers of the following questions

- How well is the current distributor performing?
- How well has the current distributor marketed Brand X?
- What is the estimate of their annual sales against annual targets?
- Is the brand happy with its current distributor?
- Can you offer a better solution that the brand is seeking?
- Most importantly, can you significantly top the sales that are being generated by the current distributor?

The answer to the above questions is not published data and requires one's human networking skills to gain the above information. Reaching out to colleagues, university, school, college friends, family, those who can get you the closest estimate of the above. Answers to these questions will help you evaluate your choice of brand, and prepare for the upcoming sales targets the brand will suggest in case they decide to be in your favor.

Region Specific Distributor

In the case of Pakistan, there are examples of brands that have distributors for specific provinces, and even different distributors for different areas in Pakistan. One pertinent example here is an international Doughnut brand that is operated by two different distribution companies, one for southern, and one for the northern region of Pakistan. As an entrepreneur, seeking a distribution license for a specific region is comparatively a more viable option than asking for nationwide distribution.

Product Specific Distributor

Product-specific distribution is also a common method for brands to license local companies based on their areas of expertise, and resources one or a few of their products from the entire portfolio. There are examples of brands such as a leading medical device company that is directly dealing in Pakistan for a few specific products, and have local distributors for the rest of their product portfolio. Compared with the other distribution licenses, a product-specific license is less complex to attain for entrepreneurs considering the choice of product is based on an entrepreneur's area of expertise, and experience.

No distributor at all

Last, and the most lucrative choice for entrepreneurs are the brands that have no representation in the desired market (Pakistan). Many lesser-known brands often reach out to established distributors through LinkedIn or Email and offer business proposals but for the reputed brand, the things are not as simple as one hopes they would be.

If a brand has no representation in the local market, at first it may sound like an easy deal to make but reputed international brands are concerned about their brand image more than the business they might generate from a new untapped market. For such similar reasons reputed brands restrain from licensing distributors which do not resonate with Brand's core values, and business policies, and practices. Hence the first step is to find if any other distributor already approached the brand, and failed to secure a license, what is the brand seeking which they couldn't provide will help you to customize your proposal accordingly. One can also research, and find Brand X distributors in neighboring countries, and gain information that you need before reaching out to Brand X.

To summarize the above, becoming a distributor of a brand that is not being distributed currently should be the preference for entrepreneurs, and to further simplify the process region-specific or product-specific licenses should be the preference for entrepreneurs. The choice of product/ region which one can later justify to Brand X based on expertise, experience, and market penetration (read PR). For a new company that lacks sales record revenue history, and experience, as an entrepreneur, you will have to leverage on your, your family's or your business partner's experience, expertise, and personal relation within the category you are going to operate in, and even from the family experience of operating business.

Entrepreneurs should build up their profile through multiple small scale start-ups they have initiated, and operated over the period, and have gained experience by those business or by the jobs they have done so far, and leverage on these when they reach out a brand for a distribution license.

Reaching out to Brands

Usually writing an email attached to a company (business) profile is how one reaches an international brand, and if there is some business exhibition or conference where you could meet, and build a reference for your upcoming email/proposal it would be a plus. Brands shortlist distribution proposal for official discussion based on the information provided by the distributor. Since there are not many chances when you are dealing with an established international brand, you must make your first impression count. Prior knowledge about what the brand seeks from its distributor will help prepare a well thought out business profile that provides all the details at the same time leveraging on the finest margin where possible. For an entrepreneur, a smart, and well thought out business profile covering all key areas will strengthen the chances for initial talks

Brands are interested in knowing your current client list, and other brands that you are associated with, and ask for evidence (distributions letters/license) for existing brands that you work with, and In some cases, Brand might ask you to have a questionnaire filled if further information is required, here is a brief view of what such a questionnaire would ask for:

Company Info

Year of establishment			Number of employees	
The number of tech. support staff			Number of sales staff	
Annual Sales		Total Capital		
Target Markets				
Items of Applicant's interest				
Info on competitors – manufacturer				
Competitor–Manufacturer		Years in Market		Remark

18. How to sell in B2C markets?

Answer to this question largely depends on what you want to sell. However, one strategy which as per an HBR article works the best is the word of mouth. Take the example of doctors, the best doctors, or their clinics in the country who do not advertise themselves. When people are sick, they ask for recommendations in their network and eventually go with the recommendation by their friends, and relatives. The growth of one's sales is organic, and the business is gradually able to increase its supply capacity as the demand increases. Often businesses advertise themselves and are unable to cater to the overwhelming demand, generating a negative word of mouth, which is lethal for the business.

Often small businesses begin by direct selling in their family, and friends, and expect to generate enough word of mouth to attract enough customers to keep them afloat. If your volumes are high enough then you may want to talk about the existing retailers, even higher then you might have to involve a distributor as explained in the previous chapter. The decision to have your outlet depends if you are not too involved in the manufacturing rather taking products from a manufacturer. Running a manufacturing unit, and then managing a retail outlet are two different ball games, and may not be done simultaneously. One needs to be outsourced to a partner. Often in a family business, different members of the family take care of the supply side, the manufacturing side, and the distribution or retailing side.

If you want to sell in multiple cities, then eventually you have to either use an e-commerce platform, or partner with retailers in multiple cities. One can also invest in making an e-commerce website, and engage a courier service for delivery, and payment collection, however, that in itself a fulltime job. Therefore outsourcing to established platforms like telemart.pk could be an option.

Before anything else, what needs to be understood is that an economic transaction only happens when a social exchange between two parties has already happened. This social exchange is the basis of the trust that must happen before any economic transaction takes place, unless the customer is too desperate, and does not have any choice other than you.

So the question again comes back to the point of how you establish your credibility with any new person, including yourself. Ask yourself what would make you trust a business or a person trying to sell you something. What he or she should demonstrate before you could consider trusting the person?

Some of the things that I would like are how the salesperson is understanding my concerns or needs, and trying to address them instead of selling me the product or service. The doctor and the car mechanic I go to are the ones who ask me to go home even when I think there is a problem, and they do not find anything wrong with me or with the car. This demonstrates that both my doctor, and my car mechanic is concerned about me, and not just making money, which they can easily do when I am already convinced if there is a problem. This sends me a very strong message about their trustworthiness.

Another very important thing is the after-sales follow up, particularly when you are selling durable goods. Call them up, or preferably text them if they are satisfied, and need any assistance with the product. Ask if they need a free checkup of their device, it would cost extra, but if that enhances the image of your company in front of them then they are very much likely to recommend it to others. I complained about a driver's behavior on one of these ride-hailing apps. Within minutes I got a phone call from their customer support, they did not just agree with my point of view, rather also returned me around 80% of the amount. Since then I am their loyal customer, despite one of their partners giving me unsatisfactory service.

Often giving your customer a little after-sales surprise in the form of a small gift for example can make lots of difference. A restaurant near my place would give goody bags to kids when the families would leave the place after dining. Further, they had a play area for kids. Because of this, my kids would never want to go anywhere else, despite the food was not as good as other places. However, these gestures could not save the restaurant as customers nevertheless go there to eat, and not have goody bags, and most customers do not have kids, implying if their food was at par with the competition, they would still be there.

So to summarize, understand what the customer wants, consider his or her interest a priority, be honest if you have something to fix or not, focus on building relationships, and not money, immediately respond to their concerns, give something extra, and do not forget to give little surprises.

19. How to sell in B2B markets[16]

Any business needs to have clientele in multiple segments. Focusing on a single segment can result in lost opportunities. The B2B segment is a very important area when it comes to selling your products. Business customers are usually high volume clients that provide you with sales revenue, and growth. Many businesses prefer to deal in the B2B segment primarily

[16] Written by Faizan Abdul Khaliq, and Razi Uddin

because focusing on a selected number of clients can provide you with significant sales volume as compared to working on each customer just to get one single unit sale in the B2C market. Several types of sellers are operating in the B2B markets, there are official distributors of imported products, and there are wholesalers, retailers that also sell to businesses, local companies that manufacture, and sell their products directly, and indenters.

When you are starting your operations in the B2B segment you must have complete knowledge about your competition that is operating in the same field and providing a similar if not the same product. You will have to counter the value proposition of your competitor otherwise you will not have many customers.

Challenges

Although the B2B sector appears to be lucrative it is much harder to tap for new businesses. The competition is tough; it is hard to gain customers, and much harder to meet all their terms, and conditions especially for a new business. Businesses are conservative when it comes to purchasing, they want to avoid risks while getting the best prices, and quality. They will prefer to deal with someone familiar unless the other party is not providing them with a value proposition that forces them to leave their old suppliers.

B2B selling requires complete documentation of sales tax, and other documentary proofs as required by the regulations for imported, and local products. Businesses will require that their supplier is a legally registered, tax-paying entity, and the product that they are procuring is genuine, and in case of imports, it is backed by tax documents stating that this product has been imported legally with all relevant taxes, and duties paid.

Almost all B2B sales are done on a credit basis therefore you must have enough reserves to support the backlog of payments while maintaining liquidity for your business. Most payments are processed 30 or 60 days post-delivery.

B2B transactions are done through banking channels, and a company account is usually used for these transactions.

It is important to have lines of credit with your suppliers so that large orders can be met without incurring the huge financial burden of making advance cash payments. This will also help you leverage your finances, and fulfill larger orders, and pay your suppliers when you get paid.

From the perspective of a new business, it must be meeting the legal, and business requirements before transitioning to the B2B segment to sustain, and succeed.

Making the sale

Although the selling in B2B is to be done to companies, and organizations instead of people there is always a human at the other end of the table in those businesses who are going to decide to buy or not buy your product. B2B selling requires reaching out and winning over the decision-maker with your value proposition. A B2B customer can be of multiple types it can be a retailer who will sell your product to customers from their stores, it can be a wholesaler who will sell your product to other retailers, it can be a hyper or supermarket, it can be an organization that requires the product for its consumption the nature of the customer will change how you will approach the decision-maker, and extract a favorable outcome from them.

Retailers, wholesalers, and markets will normally require favorable credit terms, besides, they might want discounts or supplies on short notices all of these demands must be met to close the deal. Supermarkets usually will look for flexible payment terms, and discounts on products to support their promotional sales. The organizational customer that requires product for consumption will focus more on price as compared to other aspects. You have to find and meet the needs of the customer.

Businesses will not offer the same percentage of profit that retail customers do on each sale, and B2B sellers are mindful of this fact. Since businesses purchase in bulk they expect, and demand discounts over the market price based on the volumes of their purchase, and these demands have to be catered in the B2B segment to generate large-volume of sales.

If you are a wholesaler your customers will probably be retailers who will sell your products in their stores, other than that there will be hypermarkets and superstores that will require bulk stocks. If you are a retailer that is venturing out to B2B you will be selling to other retailers or organizational customers.

B2B market dynamics

It is important to have good terms with your competition. If you are selling a product that is also sold by others a good market relationship can result in you leveraging their supplies for your orders if required. For example, you get an order to supply a large quantity of a product, and you can only fulfill a percentage of the requirement from your inventory you can fulfill the remaining quantity from the inventory of other wholesalers or retailers that are normally your customers, and or competitors this will help you keep the business, and provide sales volume to all parties involved in the sale. It will also help you to keep a modest inventory instead which is supported by your financial reserves.

How you can get an edge!

You will get an edge if you are the official distributor of a specific product that you are selling. This status provides a level of credibility, and customers know that the person selling them the product is trusted by the manufacturer to represent their product in the assigned territory. It also provides some level of satisfaction to customers that the product they will receive will be genuine.

Having large organizational customers will enable you to leverage their trust in you to gain new clients. When people see that other large buyers are trusting you enough to do business with you this makes it easier for them to consider you as their choice.

If you are dealing in products that require warranty, then the provision or facilitation of warranty claims can help you gain an edge over others this might even require you to go beyond the policy and pay out of pocket for repairs but all of this is necessary to gain, and retain the competitive edge in a marketplace where same or similar products are available for an almost similar price. For example, an official distributor will be in a better position to manage and facilitate warranty claims for the B2B customer as compared to a retailer, and retailers will have to overcome this to prevent customers from switching to the official distributor.

B2B or B2C or both

Most businesses prefer to operate on a single model which enables them to focus their energies on that particular segment. Although this strategy is successful for most businesses today businesses are transitioning to a hybrid model where they are offering services to B2B clients and diversifying operations to B2C models through subsidiaries. This helps them gain sales as well as potential tax benefits of the fixed tax regime which is expected for small, and medium-scale retailers from FBR.

Dealing with the customer

B2B customers require more personal attention, time, and focus as compared to retail customers. The interactions have to be frequent and must focus on business retention, and growth.

Wholesale or retail customers will usually be contacted through visits by the salesperson or calls. Organizations have dedicated buyers that are the point of contact for the particular category besides they can be emailed regarding offerings and sales updates. In-person, meetings are important for getting orders as well as sustaining them.

Personnel requirements B2B, and B2C

B2C usually requires salespeople at storefronts, B2B requires a POS person at hypermarkets, salesperson, and order bookers for retail, and wholesale customers, and client managers for the large clients that require more attention, and frequent interactions. For businesses that are starting operations in B2C client, management is usually done by the owner until the business reaches a stage where all operations cannot be managed by one person but initially, a single resource can be used to do sales and order booking and grow the work force with sales growth.

Appendix 1: Why we Search for Job Security. Why Not Risk Taking

By Dr. Irfan Hyder

Why are we so afraid of taking risks?
Why is our primary focus on jobs that provide security?
Why do people go after a pensionable, secure, career job?
Why do people think that becoming a government "servant" is their ultimate goal?
Why does "sarkar ki naukri" have so much premium?

An analysis of these questions takes us to the time of the early 19th century, and after the 1857 war of independence when the British Raj eliminated the land entitlements of the aristocracy. The landed aristocracy of subcontinent especially the Muslims found themselves penniless as they lost their entitlements, and their regular earnings from their land holdings disappeared. They found themselves with no marketable skills or knowledge. Their Persian language skills became worthless overnight as the official business started getting transacted in English (recall the famous saying "Farsi seekho, tael baicho").

Culturally the aristocracy of that time, especially Muslims, had looked down upon craftsmen as "kum-mi" (menial), and avoided the trades, and crafts that required working with hands. They used the terms related to crafts pejoratively, and disparagingly: Jolahay (artisan), taeli (seller of oil),kumhar (potter), qasai (meat seller), baniya (shopkeeper), mazaray (field hand), ...

Hence, they effectively shut themselves out of the businesses related to these crafts. The aristocrats or the elites, therefore, had no option but to go for English studies at the new schools/colleges so that they can eventually become government "servants". Those who did not take the modern schooling to government route, and also shut themselves out from the crafts, and trades went hungry, and their plight has been captured by several renowned poets as exemplified in the poetry, letters or life of Ghalib, Insha, etc [included still in our syllabi], and depicted by authors e.g. in the heartbreaking story of Mirza Sikandar Bakht, and included in the matric Urdu syllabus of 1977 of Sargodha Board [would someone tell me the author name?].

In short, we saw during the late 19th-century start of a mad rush towards the secure job of the British Indian Government Servant and continuing even after partition. I have seen myself official government correspondence being transacted till the late 1970s, and even into the 1980s, where the government officials would sign the official notes, and letters as "Your Most Obedient Servant"!

The safety and security of a government job (or a career job) rob you of your independence, destroys your "khudi", makes your prime duty to obey the commands, and dictation of the superior. You become like a caged parrot. He has the security of a cage. He does not need to be afraid, and continually be on the lookout for a prowling cat or a diving eagle. He has food security. He would daily get his rations in the mornings, and evenings. He has a gilded cage. He is only expected to sing, and please the master when the master so wishes. The master may reward him by taking him out of his cage for a few moments of supervised liberty but only after ensuring that the wings have been properly clipped. He has everything except the liberty to do what he wants to.

The slave mentality and the psyche so developed in the Muslims of the subcontinent was the major target of Iqbal. His metaphors of Hawk/Shaheen (who preys himself, and goes after a live prey), and denigration of vulture/kargus (who feeds on someone else's prey or dead meat") attacked this mentality.

"Woh fareeb khurda shaheen jo pala ho kargasoan may
Usay kya khabar keh kya hai, rah o rasm e shahbazi" – Iqbal

Iqbal wanted us to be shaheen who lives on the skies and does not settle down in plush homes, and Shaheen is not afraid of fluctuation of fortunes (jhapatna palatna, palat kar jhapatna) were all intended in liberating us from our love for security, safety, and official residences. However, the love for security, safety, and official residences still reign supreme in cities like Islamabad, and in particular communities.

But, then there are communities like the ferocious tribals and Afghans who could not be tamed by British. They led their lives independently, and still do. Who are enterprising, willing to work anywhere, go to any wilderness, and start from nothing with a chai-khana (tea stall) under a tree, travel all their lives on roads (driving trucks), moving from one place to another. There are desolate parts of Pakistan where you would wonder who would ever have the courage to settle and do this kind of tough work of breaking rocks, and mountains, and you will find that tribals are there doing work which no one is willing to do because it is risky and hard. British manipulative machinery tried its best to kill the spirit of these tribals by spreading jokes such as those referring to "akhroat", and "pathans", but could not. There are also settled business communities like memons, and chiniotis who are enterprising, and create their own business, and space using a trading system for their liberation. They are the real risk-takers. They have also been made a target of jokes. Unfortunately many unsuspecting from amongst us relate these jokes without understanding how they were designed to malign our psyche and mentality.

You will see a common strand among all such enterprising communities. They make their children start in a small shop or even a street stall at a very early age. They know that real learning is not in books but in real life with real people. Yes, reading, writing, and arithmetic are important and must be learned, and this a person can do in a few months or a few years starting at any age. However, the refinement of language and arithmetic skills takes place in real life. Business learning at an early age through small enterprises can lead to great things. See for example "Made in America" the autobiography of Sam Walton of Walmart who at the time of his death around 1993 was the richest man in the world.

If today after 65+ years is not the time to get out of this slave mentality, then when would it be. Unless we begin to take our destiny in our own hands, stop denigrating work, and craft, things would not change. The change is visible and is coming. We see now people looking favorably at crafts. For e.g I see in Pakistan upscale businesses with names such as "Darzi ", and "Kaarigar ", and boutiques, fashion designers (even Islamic fashion designers), Meat One, Gourmet, Nirala sweets, etc. We are rediscovering the importance of sunnah of the Prophet by reverting towards business, and trade.

The current state of affairs in Pakistan is now making us realize how difficult it is to assume responsibility, and take ownership of our destiny. But, this is the cost of real freedom.

"Apni duniya aap paida kar agar zindon mein hai" – Iqbal

About the Author: Dr. Irfan Hyder is an IT Guru, Rector at IoBM, and Founder of L2L Club.

Appendix 2: What Job Oriented Communities can learn from Memon, Delhiwala, and Chinioti entrepreneurs?

There are many communities in the country which are not known for their entrepreneurial orientation. Urdu speaking and Saraiki communities are known examples. The said communities rather look more toward job opportunities to ensure financial security. For better jobs, higher education is a prerequisite. So the people in the middle or lower classes in such communities have to look at public educational institutions to seek higher education as few can afford the hefty fees of private educational institutions. Public educational institutions, with limited capacities, and politically determined quotas, thus become a source of confrontation between different ethnic groups in the country. Government jobs are another source of confrontation between ethnic groups.

An alternative scenario also exists in the country. There are examples of various other communities who, instead of relying on jobs in the public or private sector, have been creating jobs for themselves, and others by their entrepreneurial orientation. Entrepreneurial orientation perhaps eliminates the possibility of getting into a confrontation with other ethnic groups over limited jobs available in the public or private sector. The question, therefore, is how job oriented communities can develop an entrepreneurial orientation to stop their reliance on the limited job market. To answer this question we can look at the constituents of an entrepreneurial culture among the leading entrepreneurial communities like Memon, Delhiwala, and Chinioti. Also how these cultural components can be brought into other communities.

Social capital, and Entrepreneurship

A common myth about entrepreneurship is that it requires a lot of investment. Memon, Delhiwala, and Chinioti communities on the contrary started with a very humble background. Many centuries before, all they had was (a) a strong culture of trust, (b) a will to survive in an economic atmosphere dominated by the Hindu community, and (c) a strong belief in the benevolence of their Creator. The Delhi walla community got some support from a Mughal emperor in the beginning; however, their source of livelihood was confiscated by the British establishment as a punishment for supporting the rebels in the 1857 mutiny against the British forces. The three communities survived through tough times by one critical component of their culture, that is, The spirit of trust, cooperation, and sacrifice for others. This cultural component is also referred to as 'social capital' in modern literature. European history also contains a few similar examples. Protestants, Dutch, and Jews, just to name a few, also faced difficult circumstances yet survived by virtue of a high degree of social capital. The study of European communities in history, various entrepreneurial-ethnic-groups around the world, and in Pakistan, suggests that social capital within such groups is a fundamental ingredient in the development of entrepreneurial culture.

Without social capital, the development of an entrepreneurial culture is perhaps not possible. This is because entrepreneurs need a lot of support from the people around them when they intend to start a business. A prior relationship with potential suppliers, vendors, customers, distributors, retailers, employees, partners, investors, mentors, etc. makes it a whole lot easier. A customer you already know might give you confidence that if the product/service is at the right price, right quality, and delivered at the right time, then he or she would purchase. A supplier may offer supplies on credit, while employees who trust in you, may wait for a few days in case if you fail to pay salary on time. Investors may invest not just because they want to support, but also because they have trust in your character, and that you may not disappear with the money, also because it is not just your credibility, but the credibility of your entire family which is at stake. Now as the business paddles ahead, the continuous support from all the stakeholders makes it much easier for the entrepreneur. Now imagine if the stakeholders do not trust each other, or not willing to cooperate. How would that facilitate each other? Trust is the fundamental lubricant of any market, which allows the flow of capital, and resources between stakeholders; it is not the other way around.

How to develop social capital?

How social capital and subsequent entrepreneurial orientation can be developed in a community? To answer this we may look at the experience of local entrepreneurial communities. The experience of Memon, Delhiwala, and Chinioti in this regard is not very different from their European counterparts as mentioned above. Their experience suggests that a strong religious orientation among community members provides the basic motivation for cooperative behavior and entrepreneurial orientation. There are many examples from the tradition of the Prophet s.a.w, and the life of Sahaba-e-kiram r.a which encourage self-employment, which can be referred to as the first step on the path of entrepreneurship. Islamic Belief in God as the provider of sustenance can make a believer less risk-averse, collaborative behavior encouraged by Islam can foster trust, and fear of Day of Judgment can prevent Muslim entrepreneurs from betraying commitments in the market. So for a Muslim community, the first encouragement toward cooperative behavior, and entrepreneurship emerges right from their belief system.

The concerned in job oriented communities need to evaluate if such a culture of trust, cooperation, and sacrifice persist in their community? Assuming if it does not, then working on enhancing the religious orientation of the community member may help. Practicing Muslims are more likely to cooperate, and sacrifice for others, and honor their commitments for the sake of reward on the Day of Judgment, while such behavior makes them appear more trustworthy among stakeholders.

The practical use of social capital increases social capital. When a person honors his commitment to stakeholders, cooperates with others, then such behavior typically increases the level of trust between two people. There is a saying in Urdu language 'tali dono hatho se bajti hai', which means it takes two hands to clapage Therefore, more stakeholders indulging in trustworthy, and cooperative behavior can trigger a virtuous cycle subsequently increasing the likelihood of such behavior in future. The spirit of cooperation, and sacrifice among the family members (usually brothers) working together in the same business is pivotal to the success of a family business, and survival during tough times.

Sometimes the level of trust in a community drops so low that cooperative behavior raises eyebrows, and people even begin to question the intentions of a person cooperating with others. If so happens, then a practicing Muslim needs to recall that doubting other's intentions (bad-gumani) is strictly discouraged by Prophet s.a.w. Furthermore, backbiting (gheebat), and making a baseless accusation behind someone's back (bohtan) are grave sins. In a community where such social ills exist, developing a culture of trust is difficult. More religious education about desirable, and undesirable habits, therefore, is important to increase the level of social capital among the community members. The upbringing of children by the parents and family members is also critical in the development of desirable behavior.

The Motivation for Entrepreneurship

Social capital is a fundamental ingredient of an entrepreneurial culture; however, it may not be the key driver toward entrepreneurship. Likewise, the belief that Allah s.w.t is the sole provider of sustenance also may ease the fear of risk, but may not push a person to start a venture. The push or motivation toward an entrepreneurial orientation can be of intrinsic or extrinsic nature. Teachings of Islam do provide some intrinsic motivation. For example:

A hadith suggests that 9/10 parts of rizq are provided by Allah s.w.t to the traders in the market, while the only 1/10th is for the labor class. Furthermore, doing business is Sunnah of the Prophet s.a.w, and Sahaba-e-kiram r.a.

Research (published in Harvard Business Review) also suggests that a businessman or an entrepreneur may also live a more ideologically independent life as compared to an employee. Employees often have to agree with the values or beliefs of their employers to improve their job prospects. This may not be the case of entrepreneurs if they are not highly dependent on someone like an investor.

Islam also does not discourage its followers to strive for financial security in a legitimate way Islam discourages toward choosing a life where one is at the risk of begging for help from others. To ensure financial security for oneself, and family, a person may want to put his or her eggs in multiple baskets. It means starting multiple ventures or diversifying one's portfolio of investments over some time may enhance a person's financial security. This is very much possible for an entrepreneur, however, difficult - if not impossible - for an employee.

On the other hand, extrinsic motivation can emerge due to the threats in the external world. For example, the lack of employment opportunities. The Chinioti community, for example, was dependent on the Hindu community almost a century before, as Hindu were dominating in every business. But some members of the Chinioti community observed that Hindu do not touch animal hides due to religious reasons. Hides were converted into leather, a raw material for a variety of goods like shoes, and bags. A few entrepreneurs from the Chinioti community experimented with dealing in hides and started in a very humble way. This turned out to be a road toward immense fortune for the pioneering entrepreneurs in the Chinioti community. Looking at the success of a few, the rest also got motivated and ventured into the leather business with the help of the pioneers. After a few generations, they have diversified in a variety of fields. For more details, please see the book 'Kamyab Log' by Dr. Amjad Saqib.

How to start?

The answer to this question would depend on your age. For example, consider a person in 40s who is already employed, has a family to support, kids going to school, a kitchen to run, etc, with no other financial support;

such a person would be risk-averse. However, the same person may have the market experience, necessary level of maturity, contacts, credibility, some savings to invest which may help him or her to initiate something, depending on how street smart a person is. Someone much younger, perhaps in his teens or early 20s, unmarried, may not have financial pressures (if his or her family is financially stable) and can experiment starting something, however, he or she may lack the necessary experience, level of maturity, contacts, and credibility, and may have to borrow money from his parents or elders.

If we look at Memon, Delhiwala, and Chinioti, we see that their path toward entrepreneurship began perhaps very early. At the age of 14-15, the boys particularly are encouraged to spend time in their father's business, or business of a relative, or a family friend, etc. Often teenagers spend a few hours every day running a business, generally doing odd jobs. They are also encouraged to spend much of their summer vacations likewise. By the time a boy reaches his 20s, he already has many years of market experience and has learned the tricks of the trade. Furthermore, they have the full moral support of their family if they want to initiate something on their own after gaining many years of experience.

For job oriented communities, this is perhaps difficult to digest. They would want their children to only focus on their formal education, which is considered fundamentally important to secure admission in a reputable university, which is believed to be a prerequisite to get a good job. However, entrepreneurial communities that are not dependent on the job market for financial security may not consider formal education as a matter of life and death. So if as a parent you are willing to support your children to become entrepreneurs, you may also encourage them to spend time in a running business (smaller is better), so they may learn the tricks of the trade first hand. However, for this to happen, you must personally know a businessman or an entrepreneur who is willing to accommodate your boy and provide him the necessary training.

For the person who is married, and has financial obligations toward his family, who now wants to start a business, might want to check if he or she already knows a customer. Many Memon, Delhiwala, Chinioti already know a willing customer before taking the risk. All they have to do is to make sure that they fulfill the customer's expectations so ensure repeat sales. This is exactly where the prior relationship with the potential suppliers, vendors, potential employees, partners, investors, mentors, etc. may become handy. An employed person may take leave from his job for a couple of weeks, and try to engage all the potential stakeholders to ensure a sale. But taking a leave may not be required at all in some cases. It might be very much possible to fulfill a customer's requirement in your free hours after the job or on your weekend. Once you see customers coming back, and even bringing more customers by referring you to others, then you might think of leaving your full-time job if the returns are promising. To summarize, the following questions you might want to ask from yourself:

- Do I have the necessary skills/experience in the domain?
- Do I have the necessary contacts with the right vendors, suppliers, distributors, customers, and do they also trust me?
- Do I know people who I can hire?
- Can I satisfy customer needs/wants using my skill, experience, connections, contacts, and other resources?
- Can I satisfy some customers without investing, or investing the only 1/10th of the financial resources I have?

Is my family willing to support me in the process of making the jump toward starting my own business, will they back me up for a while in case I collapse?

If you are working in a small or medium-sized business, and if you have good terms with the owner, then you might look for an opportunity to get into partnership over a new venture which your employer might want to start but do not have the necessary time to do so. Your employer can also be your first customer. A student entrepreneur of mine had an employee who would cut potatoes for French fries for his small food outlet. The boy instead decided to sell my student potato strips, he even asked for a small investment from my student (his employer) which he provided happily. In a few months, he was supplying large quantities to many food outlets, and restaurants, earning a handsome amount per month. Now the sky's the limit for him. There are many such examples.

Frugal Lifestyle, Organic Growth, and Communal Support

The habit of a frugal lifestyle, encouraged by the teaching of Islam, also followed by the elders of Memon, Delhiwala, and Chinioti communities in general (the new generation is these communities are perhaps leaving this habit), can be referred to as 'fundamental' to successfully walk on the path of entrepreneurship. Robert Kiyosaki is among the modern advocates of this habit for entrepreneurs. Kiyosaki suggests that an entrepreneur must avoid spending on any asset which does not yield any return to the extent possible. A frugal lifestyle allows an entrepreneur to avoid spending on any unnecessary expenses, particularly luxuries while reinvesting some of his savings back into the business, and keeping the rest for an uncertain future. The Memon community is particularly known, even mocked due to their frugal habits. Those who mock, perhaps fail to understand the deep wisdom behind this habit. The modern followers of Minimalism and Stoic philosophy (which includes top entrepreneurs of Silicon Valley) on the contrary would fully understand the wisdom behind a Memon's attitude toward spending on necessities only.

It must be noted that the personal expense of an entrepreneur's lifestyle or the lifestyle adopted by his or her dependents, is a cost of business he or she owns. According to a Chinioti entrepreneur, by keeping their expenses to the bare minimum, Memon today still can outperform the Chinioti entrepreneurs in the market. The money saved by avoiding unnecessary expenses not just at a personal level, but also while doing business (like maintaining a luxurious office even if it does not add any value to the business), can be reinvested in the business, or can provide a safety net to the entrepreneur in case business suffers some kind of a loss. Reinvestment of profits also saves an entrepreneur from approaching a bank whose involvement is also found to be paradoxically detrimental for business growth. All entrepreneurs I interviewed from Memon, Delhiwala, and Chinioti community shared a similar concern. Recently a friend working with entrepreneurs in Sialkot also shared a similar observation.

An entrepreneur, who does not owe to a bank, or any informal investor, who also has been able to sufficiently save, is more capable of facilitating new entrepreneurs or the ones in trouble. A culture of frugality widespread in an entrepreneurial community can better facilitate other entrepreneurs within or even outside the community.

Indirectly a culture of frugality can also contribute to maintaining social capital. The social relationship between family members, relatives, and even community members can become competitive in a material sense, with a culture of auspicious consumption of luxury items. The resources at the disposal of community members, which were used to facilitate each other, maybe diverted toward raising the so-called standard of living. As a result class consciousness may spread, competition may often turn into conflicts, subsequently weakening the social bonding, and the spirit to cooperate, and sacrifice within the community members. The reduction of cooperation and sacrifice may also end up reducing the level of trust. A culture of frugality is crucial to maintain a high degree of social capital in a community.

Therefore, a job-oriented community that intends to turn entrepreneurial may also look into its spending habits. Competition to get ahead in material consumption may harm entrepreneurial success. The social relations which are fundamental to entrepreneurial success may also be weakened in the process.

Final thoughts

A question that has not been sufficiently answered so far is who is going to bring this change within the job oriented communities? The answer is 'you' if you happen to be a part of the communities. This you may do by (a) setting an example by following the suggestions mentioned above, and if you are too old then encouraging the young ones in your family toward starting their venture, (b) by initiating a discussion, and sharing business ideas with the community members, (c) sharing this article, even translate it if possible, or similar ones within your network, (d) finding like-minded people who can keep reminding each other, etc.

Cultural transformation is an intergenerational process. Many from the job oriented communities which I meet frequently are already convinced to walk on an entrepreneurial path, all that they need is perhaps some moral support from the elders in their family. On the contrary, the new generation of the Memon, Delhiwala, and Chinioti communities are becoming job oriented. Some business owners in these communities are not even hopeful that their generations-old family business would survive after them as their children are more interested to carry it forward. This would eventually leave gaps in the market in the coming years. Perhaps entrepreneurs from job-oriented communities can fill in the gaps, or let the Chinese avail the developing opportunity.

The future depends on the choices we make today. If we intend to secure the financial future of our upcoming generation, the answer perhaps lies in becoming self-reliant by walking the path of entrepreneurship. The living examples in entrepreneurial communities can provide immense learning opportunities. If we want to remain hopelessly dependent on public, and private institutions to keep creating jobs for us, then it's up to us. However, if we want to take charge of our destinies, then the choice is again ours.

Appendix 3: How Memon, Delhiwala, and Chinioti Starts a Venture

The following steps are taken from my paper 'How Memon, Delhi Saudagaran, and Chinioti Entrepreneurs Create New Ventures?' to be published in the Oct 2019 issue of Pakistan Business Review. The complete paper can be read on my academia or research gate profile.

Step 1: Evaluate yourself, ask what I know, whom I know, who am I, what I have, and what my passions are. Identify means, and do not go beyond them. Know the bird in hand. The knowledge, capital, family workforce, infrastructure support, the connections with stakeholders in the network, goodwill of the family are all resources. Gradually expand by investing the profits. Do not take excessive risks as they increase the chances of failure. Experimentation can be done to test new ideas by leveraging the resources available in the support network.

Step 2: Seek advice from the elders regarding the opportunities which exist in the domain of one's expertise. Knowing the customer in advance reduces the risk of investment significantly. Often opportunities emerge in the process of building a business, sometimes in the form of accidents or unprecedented events.

Step 3: Get experience as an apprentice or an employee in someone else's business; market experience can also be gained through brokerage which would also generate returns. Knowledge about the product, production process, competition, and customer is fundamental before starting a business. Working in a smaller business is more beneficial as it is possible to learn about the entire supply chain which is not visible in large scale enterprises.

Step 4: Do not invest all the savings or the money borrowed from father or someone else, have something as a backup in case the business collapses. Work out the affordable loss, and invest only that amount. Keep the cost low, and work with your hand as much as possible.

Step 5: Build credibility with the suppliers, and goodwill with the customers. Market reputation is one of the important assets an entrepreneur possesses. Commitment to the customer must be honored at all costs. Timely payments to the supplier build trust and the supplier comes forward with easier credit terms.

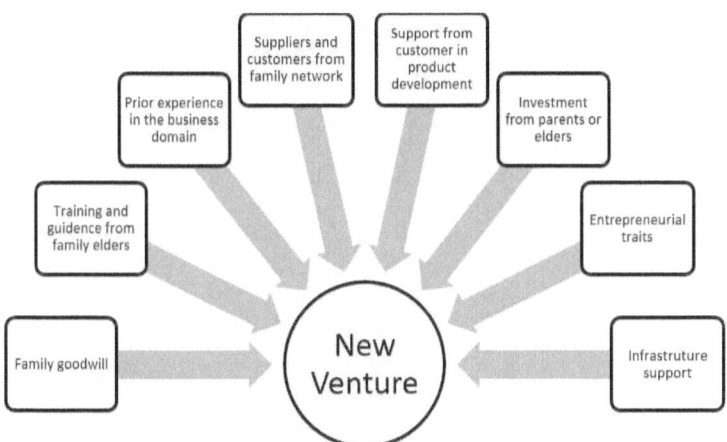

Step 6: Expansion is done within the means. Banks are avoided. Partnership with trustworthy community members, friends, or close relatives is sought. Customers are sought from the network of family, and community. Employees are hired using community references. A family-like atmosphere is recommended to keep the employees loyal, and motivated.

The same criterion of meritocracy is applied for all participating members including the immediate family, relatives, and employees from within, and outside the community.

www.ingramcontent.com/pod-product-compliance
Lightning Source LLC
Chambersburg PA
CBHW030633220526
45463CB00004B/1504